Where the
RIGHT
went
WRONG
on
National
Security

★ ★ ★ ★ ★

(and the Left too)

Andre Michael
Eggelletion

Where the
RIGHT
went
WRONG
on
National
Security

★ ★ ★ ★ ★

(and the Left too)

Andre Michael
Eggelletion

MILLIGAN BOOKS   BOOKS   CALIFORNIA

Published and Distributed by:
Milligan Books, Inc.

Cover Layout & Design by: Linda D. Tidwell
Gary Scott

Cover Photo by:
Greg Roland: skyfirecap@bellsouth.net

Interior Formatting by:
Linda D. Tidwell: lt@ltidwelldesigns.com

First Printing, March 2006
10 9 8 7 6 5 4 3 2 1

ISBN: 0-9771082-5-2

Milligan Books, Inc.
1425 W. Manchester Ave., Suite C
Los Angeles, California 90047
www.milliganbooks.com
(323) 750-3592

Andre Michael Eggelletion
www.talktoandre.com
talktoandrenow@hotmail.com

Contents

This book is dedicated to the innocent men, women, and children of this planet who have suffered and died under conditions associated with America's national security policies.

About the Author

Andre Michael Eggelletion is the host of the nationally syndicated *Andre Eggelletion Show*, airing Monday through Friday, 11 a.m. to 1 p.m. EST on the Information Radio Network, which is broadcast online at www.talktoandre.com. Each day, Andre brilliantly probes the current and historical events that have helped shape our lives, while engaging his listeners in lively and enlightening discussions. His commentary is refreshingly intelligent, thought-provoking, and entertaining.

Andre is one of the few successful African-American personalities in national syndication today. His highly acclaimed book, *Thieves in the Temple: America Under the Federal Reserve System*, has made Eggelletion one of the nation's leading commentators on the Fed and the global economy. He is the only known African-American in U.S. history to publish a book on the subject. This fact is important, but it is truly overshadowed by the eloquence and passion with which he speaks to all Americans on not only the Fed and national security, but on an extremely wide pallet of political, economic, and social issues from a global perspective.

This latest effort on the development of the national security state reveals how it has led to the rise of an imperial presidency in America and reveals the profound affect on the lives of every living thing on the planet. It is as compelling as it is timely. Andre is available for radio interviews and speaking engagements nationwide.

Visit Andre online at www.talktoandre.com

Acknowledgments

First, I must acknowledge the ultimate source, the infinite and immaculate pure spirit substance that inspired me to write this book. I pray that I, and this book, will be of some help to mankind and remind us of the need to choose right over wrong.

Second, there is a host of individuals who have affected my life in significant ways, to whom I owe a debt of gratitude. They, too, have enabled me to develop my thoughts and accomplish my goals. To begin with, I would like to thank my parents, Mr. and Mrs. Josephus and Annie Lee Eggelletion. For over 62 years, they have shared a boundless love and dedication to each other, their seven children, their grandchildren, and great-grandchildren.

I also thank and acknowledge the rest of my family: My wife, Deborah, for her deep love and support. I love you, baby doll; my brother, Broward County Commissioner Josephus Eggelletion Jr., for being a steadfast instrument of God and greatly enhancing the quality of life for present and future generations of Floridians for over 18 years; my sisters, Jean, Loretta, Josephine, Carolyn, Treva, and all their children and grandchildren; and lastly, all my in-laws and their families. I love you all.

A special thanks to the employees of Eggelletion Enterprises: Carl, Derrick, Geoffery, Shenita, Sandra, Carla, and the many others through the years who have assisted and influenced me. I couldn't do any of this without your loyal dedication.

An extra special thanks to Bill Armstrong and David Rich, president and vice-president of the Armstrong Ford and Toyota of Homestead (www.armstrongcars.com). Both of you are a sterling example of excellence and an exceptional role model for all to follow. I love you both.

To everyone at Poller and Jordan Advertising (www.pjadv.com): Bob, Mike, Rick, Joe, and the girls. You guys are awesome. Everyone at Carrera and Associates (www.carreraadvertising.com): Nick, Steve, Lisa, Brian, and everyone there. Keep up the good work.

Also special thanks to Carl Nelson, one of the greatest talk-show hosts in America, for teaching me the meaning of the word "broadcasting," and to his beautiful wife, Lyndah Hudson, for unleashing my talents on the world. I love and owe you both a great debt.

Words cannot express my deepest thanks to a true friend, Joe Meyer (www.meyerassoc.com). The way you have selflessly extended your helping hand to me will never be forgotten. You are a great role model, inspiration, and a consummate professional. If everyone in the world had just one tenth of your character, integrity, knowledge, and fortitude, this planet would be so much better.

To Dr. Larry Bates and Chuck Bates: I never would have thought two staunch Republicans would be the first to say to me, "Have a seat at our table." You both are a bright beacon of light in conservative America. The network you started, the Information Radio Network (www.inforadionet.com), and everyone there are truly making an indispensable contribution to the greatness of this nation.

God bless you all for the kindness, professionalism, and support you have shown to me. I am deeply grateful.

To Brad Saul and the Matrix Media family (www. matrixmediainc.com), thank you for believing in me and for your diligent efforts in affiliate relations. We're going all the way because you guys are simply the best.

To all the radio and television shows across this great nation that have embraced me: *Coast to Coast AM*/George Noory, Art Bell, Lisa Lyon. *New York 1 News*, Time Warner's 24-hour newschannel in NYC with Jennifer Madden. KJLH and *Front Page*/Stevie Wonder, Carl Nelson, Earl Ofari Hutchinson, Dominique Diprima, Rob, and the rest of the family. *The Alex Jones Show* with Alex Jones, www.infowars.com. *America at Night* with Katie Delaney, Dave DeBatto, Jeff Dorf, and Mike Elmore. *The Power Hour* with Capt. Joyce Riley and Dave Von Kleist. *Wing TV* with Victor Thorn. *Ahead of the Trend* with Jim Puplava and Ike Iossif. *Market Views TV* with Ike Iossif. *The Midas Report* with Darrell Smith.

I also wish to thank the following radio and television stations: *Wise Trade* with Tony Marino. *Premier Trade, The Opening Bell, and Afternoon Rap on the James Dicks Financial Network with Jack Lott. The Concord Forex Group* and my mentor Don Snellgrove, www.cfgtrading.com. Republic Broadcasting Network and the *John Stadtmiller Show. The Lou Epton Show. Radio Liberty* with Dr. Stan Montieth. *The Bill Braumbaur Show. The Mike Slattery Show. The Rain of Truth Show* with Dr. Rain Morgan. *The Bill Meyers Show. Drive Time Dialog* with Armstrong Williams and Alan Combs. *The*

Dan Savino Show. The Edge with Daniel Ott. *Frankly Speaking* with Frank Whalen. *Freedom Law School* with Peymon Mottahedeh. *Free World Alliance* with Anthony Hilder. *The Tom Pope Show. The American Free Press. The Communicators* with Leroy Baylor WHCR FM 90.3 *The Voice of Harlem* Web site www.whcr.org. *The Maxine Thompson Show. The Brent Clanton Show, KXYZ Business Radio. The Jeff Buchorary Show. The Truman Berst Show. Memphis Real Talk* with Jennings Bernard, www.memphisrealtalk.com. The *Dr. Firpo Carr Show,* Progressive Talk 1190 AM, Los Angeles.

Special thanks to a wonderful photographer, Greg Roland, who did the cover photo for my book, skyfirecap@bellsouth.net. Undoubtedly I have left out a few so please forgive me and know that I thank you all regardless. To all the wonderful guests on the *Andre Eggelletion Show,* thank you for a great conversation.

Finally, to my publisher Milligan Books, Inc., (www.milliganbooks.com); Dr. Rosie Milligan and staff, you are the best. Rosie, you have been at the vanguard of black literary excellence. Let me take this moment to recognize your indispensable contribution to the greatness of not only black America, but also this nation on a whole. I owe you a great debt of gratitude. May you continue to shine as one of our brightest stars. And a special thanks to my graphic artist, the very beautiful and talented Linda Tidwell (lt@tidwelldesigns.com), for her tireless and professional efforts in making my books look so great. You are the best at what you do, and it shows. You are simply awesome. Thanks, Alanna Boutin, for a wonderful job editing; alanna_boutin@sil.org. My thanks also to my promoters, Pam Reimer with *Guest Talk*, Ilene Proctor and Murray Rubin — you both have been a blessing. If I missed anyone, please forgive me. I love you all.

Introduction

I find it sad that time and time again, conservatives in America allow themselves to be duped by hawks in the government into taking on all kinds of problems. They often accept generalized and inductive arguments when agreeing to unilateral executive policies in the name of national security. They don't take proper time to deductively scrutinize their party's policies before endorsing them. The Left is often guilty of the same thing as well. Things like spying on the U.S. population without a warrant or any oversight, secret detention camps, torture, the dismantling of alliances, intolerable border policies, and other activist government policies that favor the elite few over the increasingly irrelevant many are accepted.

Very few people understand the weight of the political, economic, strategic, social, and even spiritual compromises we place upon ourselves and our neighbors throughout the developing world in the name of our national security. This is partly because some right-wing elements in our news media, being compromised by the profits they receive from major corporations with their political axes to grind, only give us a very carefully skewed view of our world. They carefully provide only enough information to allow Americans to consistently formulate maligned inductive conclusions about our foreign policy and its global ramifications. In other words, we end up believing exactly what those institutions and individuals, who use the national security state apparatus to advance a plutocratic agenda, want us to believe.

Since 1947, the abrasive policies of the National Security Council, which has primarily been Republican-controlled, have created the greatest risks to our national security. We are not aware of how often the weight of America's interests under the national security mandate produces intrusive and sometimes catastrophic consequences for our neighbors, and ultimately, ourselves. We must understand how the by-product of executive actions carried out in the name of national security so often end up creating chaos and anti-Americanism around the world. We must not allow the hegemonic aspirations of the moneyed few, who, through their lobbyists, own the Republicans in Washington, make this nation appear to others as if it serves itself like a blind dog in a meat house.

To better understand the paradoxical nature of the national security state, we must go beyond inductive scrutiny, which has led many to falsely conclude that the invocation of the "national security" mandate is always done with a humanistic intent. In this book, we will deductively and analytically examine what's done in the dark in the name of America's national security interests. Then, hopefully, you will see how the political Right is so often wrong on national security.

But Democrats have made mistakes on national security issues as well. The difference, as history has shown, is that Democrats seem to learn better from their mistakes. Although the lopsided quid pro quo relationship with Saudi Arabia began under a Democrat for pragmatic purposes rather than correcting its weaknesses, Republicans have subsequently cultivated it to America's strategic and economic detriment. It was a right-wing national security mandate that carried out the overthrow of the government in Iran in 1953, Guatemala in 1954, and Chile in 1973. It was a right-wing national security council that brought us the Iran/Contra Affair. It was a right-wing national security council that stood by and watched the collapse of the Soviet Union without being properly prepared for the post-cold war strategic environment. It was a far right-wing national security state apparatus that brought us the current war in Iraq with its associated domestic compromises to freedom, privacy, and dissent in America. In short, the national security state is a wild, untamed beast under the direction of Republicans. Time and time again, we find ourselves sacrificing peace in the name of maintaining peace. Time after time, those positive attributes of America that previous generations have struggled to maintain have been sacrificed under the mania of right-wing national security doctrines.

How did all of this get started? The National Security Council started out in 1947 as a civilian advisory council to the President of the United States. By the time of the Reagan administration, it became the epicenter for illegal, covert military operations, including coups, proxy wars, illegal arms deals, and drug running.

Quite frankly, I don't see how some Republicans can say that they love America and dismiss cries for justice against the constitutional crisis that was associated with the Iran/Contra Affair during the Reagan administration as just more leftist bomb-throwing at a great President! How can they excuse the wanton violations of our civil liberties by the current Bush administration's ignoring of the Foreign Intelligence Surveillance Act (FISA) court and illegally spying on Americans? Are they that institutionalized in their thinking? Are they so blinded by their conservative ideology that they are willing to give a pass to the mayhem and chaos that these kinds of black operations being back-doored out of the White House invariably create? Are they willing to deem the sacrifice of so many brave Americans who died for these freedoms as null and void?

Our nation is diminished when it instigates coups, overthrows governments, and implements other reckless covert activity in the name of national security. We must acknowledge that sometimes the way we pursue our national security interests helps to create enemies of not only the government, but also the citizens of the United States of America. We must acknowledge that no one, not even the President during times of war, is above the law. Are my brothers and sisters on the Right too pious to see it, or are they just that naïve? Are they all that indifferent, or are they simply too fearful to say anything about it?

I marvel at how we fail to recognize that events like these are a major abuse of executive privilege in America. In other words, these events should have revealed the fact that unilateral executive power under the national security mandate can be abused. But like I said, the Republicans don't learn from history too well. I strongly feel that if they had learned their lesson and the country had done more to teach them a lesson after Iran/Contra, the current, unwarranted, unilateral preemptive war in Iraq would never have materialized.

But we haven't learned our lesson. What we have done is allowed some Republicans to commit the same type of Iran/Contra era, Watergate era, and FBI counterintelligence programs (COINTELPRO) era abuse of power all over again in the name of national security. Once again, we have allowed the application of unwarranted unilateralism under the administration of another compromised Republican U.S. President. This time, rather than just trashing the U.S. Constitution in the process, these neo-conservatives (neo-cons) have rendered significant damage to the Transatlantic Alliance and our image abroad. In a world where the grisly attacks of terrorists have become an international problem, they have alienated badly needed friends and sacked our own ability to keep tabs on the shadowy, stateless activity of terrorists.

Just as the will of the American people, the will of Congress as expressed through the Boland Amendment, and the Constitution of the United States were totally disregarded in favor of covert and illegal assistance to the Contras by the Reagan/Bush White House, likewise, the will of the American people, the will of Congress, and the U.S. Constitution were subverted and compromised by the wanton disregard for credible intelligence on Iraqi Weapons of Mass Destruction (WMD) programs. There was little or no substantive attempt by the Bush White House to first verify the intelligence gathered by UN inspectors, Ambassador Joseph Wilson, and others, then formulate policy accordingly before presenting their argument for going to war with Iraq. Instead, once again, we were told that this action had to be taken in the name of national security, and as far as these neo-cons were concerned, that's all we needed to know. Once that justification was invoked, it provided the basis for this unjustified, unilateral, executive action, and, once again, the consequences have been troublesome.

17

All of this doesn't mean that we should not engage in military action to insure the safety of innocent people in this age of terrorism. Peace, safety, and stability in the strategic order of the world should be the objective of any national security strategy. But in the case of the deeply flawed and problematic war in Iraq, the National Security Act of 1947 was, again, abused. Simply put, the war in Iraq was one of the greatest strategic blunders in U.S. history. In an interview with former Senator Carol Mosley Braun, the senator summed up the strategic difficulty and reckless tactical approach of the Bush administration. She said that attacking Iraq "amounted to taking a baseball bat to a hornet's nest" (South Florida Speaks Out 2004).

Many people all over the U.S. no longer believe in President Bush's strategy of "fighting them there so that we don't have to face them here in America." In fact, many Americans have always felt that the reason Iraq was chosen as the first battleground in the war on terrorism was to secure Western control of its oil. I do agree that oil and flat-out greed are the culprits, but only in part. I believe that wars are very complex things, and there are many reasons for the genesis of war. In the case of the current war in Iraq, I view it, also in part, as an outgrowth of the Cold War with the Soviet Union.

As for oil, in order to fully understand what factor it played, you must take a look at the history of U.S. presidential policies on strategic petroleum reserves from 1945 to the present. The development of U.S. strategies to maintain control of the Persian Gulf region and its resources was critical during the Cold War, and it colors the current so-called war against terrorism. After reading this book, you should more clearly see how nations are pitted against each other in a dangerous drive toward their different visions of a New World Order.

Make no mistake about it — facilitating the West's strategic petroleum interests during the Cold War had a tremendous geo-political ripple effect. It has always been linked to the U.S. dollar's hegemony and to its status as a reserve currency. Making sure oil has remained a dollar-backed commodity has largely defined long-standing U.S. presidential policies on strategic petroleum reserves. In short, whoever controls the world's dwindling oil reserves will be in the position to control and exploit the development of other nations, including China's development. This has been a great race between the United States, Russia, and the rest of the industrialized nations of the world. During the 1940s, Professor Carroll Quigley, in his book, Tragedy and Hope, said,

> It would appear at the present time that new civilizations may be in the throes of birth in Japan, possibly in China, less likely in India, and dubiously in Turkey or Indonesia. The birth of a powerful civilization at any or several of these points would be of primary significance in world history, since it would serve as a counter balance to the expansion of Soviet civilization on the landmass of Eurasia (Quigley 1966).

Nicholas Lardy in an article entitled "Integrating China into the Global Economy" and Bill Powell in an article entitled "China's Great Step Forward; Get Ready for the Biggest Coming Out Party in the History of Capitalism: China's Formal Accession to the WTO. Here's How the Global

Economy Is Going to Change" assess how the global economy would change after China's ascension to the World Trade Organization. Both authors describe this event as "the biggest coming out party in the history of capitalism."

The war in Iraq is largely being fought to ensure that Western interests will control and exploit the rate, pace, and sequence of the near-developed world's future economic and industrial development. A prerequisite in achieving that goal requires maintaining the U.S. dollar's hegemony and control of Iraq's strategically vital petroleum reserves. That's why we were fed the erroneous WMD story. It provided the political and strategic mandate necessary to allow the invocation of unilateral options under the auspices of national security.

Likewise, dollar hegemony, and its influence on the lives of the poor, is just as profound. I believe that the American dollar is in peril, in no small part, due to the costs of contemporary geo-political uncertainty created by national security blunders. Not facing and addressing that fact will have dire economic consequences for the United States.

As an article entitled "The Passing of the Buck" *(The Economist 2004)* reveals, the collapse of the dollar's status as the world's currency reserve will have a notable effect upon this nation and the world. The article states: "A slow, steady shift out of dollars could perhaps be handled. But if America continues to show such neglect of its own currency, then a fast-falling dollar and rising American interest rates would result. It will be how far and how fast the dollar falls that determines the future for America's economy and the world's."

For this reason, the world's central banks have the responsibility of applying effective countermeasures that will help safely steer the markets and maintain economic order, not withstanding the fact that, collectively, peaceful nations do have the right to repel any attempt from rogue states at unleashing the economic equivalent of a nuclear bomb upon its neighbors. But going it alone to achieve this goal is dangerous. There should be an international consensus and effort to counter weapons of mass destruction (economic and otherwise). Should a single nation take on this charge, especially when done ambiguously through deception, it will be viewed as totalitarian.

Thus, in the final analysis, the temptation afforded to American presidents under the national security mandate to exercise illegal actions in pursuing hegemonic aspirations is extremely great. The stakes are high in today's competitive environment over evaporating resources. They define the new strategic order of the world. That's why incidents occur, such as the Iran/Contra Affair 20 years ago, with the accompanying covert and illegal activity of the White House, the National Security Council, and the CIA that stoked the fires of war in Nicaragua between the Contra rebels and the Sandinista Army. These should have been avoided. A handful of men in the Reagan/Bush White House, operating under the cloak of national security, actually formed a shadow government. Their illegal activity was nothing short of totalitarianism. According to Senator John Kerry,

> They were willing to literally put the Constitution at risk because they believed somehow in a higher order of things, that the end is justified by

the means. That's the most Marxist totalitarian doctrine I've ever heard of in my life. If you can have a retired colonel, you know, in mufti, running around, making deals in other countries on their own, soliciting funds to overthrow governments, and hide it from the American people so you have no accountability, you have done the very thing that James Madison and others feared most when they were struggling to put the Constitution together, which was to create an accountable system which didn't have runaway power, which didn't concentrate power in one hand so that you could have one person making a decision and running off against the will of the American people (Moyers 1988).

But what's different this time is that this situation in Iraq has augmented, not diminished, real threats to the strategic and economic well-being of the West. From a strategic perspective, a failure in Iraq would have a destabilizing ripple around the world. From an economic perspective, the global economy is extremely vulnerable to geo-political uncertainty. And the situation in Iraq is making it worse. Saddam's attempts to shift dollar reserves and force oil into becoming a Euro-backed commodity would have caused a tremendous global economic disruption. But the lack of a more international approach in dealing with terrorism has also raised the potential of the same kinds of complications.

Bush didn't have to lie; the truth may have worked just fine. The world might have given consent to a more unified and pragmatic response to the attacks of 911. Virtually the entire world was sympathetic to U.S. security concerns immediately following those attacks. But what happened? The political Right in America chose the doctrine of unilateralism over statesmanship and diplomatic internationalism. The President told the world, "Either you're with us, or you're with the terrorists." He thumbed his nose at the Transatlantic Alliance when we needed it the most. He ignored past treaties, which were forged in blood. He alienated America in the world.

In the final analysis, the administration's preemptive military actions, based on false allegations of a reconstituted WMD program in Iraq posing an eminent threat to the United States and the world, without irrefutable proof, was only made possible under the national security mandate. In short, abuses of the National Security Act have allowed an imperial presidency to materialize in America today.

Chapter One

★ ★ ★ ★ ★

The Development of the National Security Council
The National Security Act of 1947

President Harry S. Truman signed the National Security Act into law on July 26, 1947. With a stroke of his pen, he established unprecedented powers within the Presidency. This would significantly expand the President's ability to execute his oath to support, protect, and defend the Constitution of the United States. This would also increase the potential for the highest office in this government of, by, and for the people, to be transformed into the command post of a self-serving shadow government. Sadly, that stroke of Truman's pen has sometimes brought election rigging, counterfeit mobs in the street, drug running, proxy wars, political assassination, and revolution. The fact that this has sometimes been the sullen by-product of the almost unlimited executive privilege under the National Security Act of 1947 is largely unknown to the American people.

The kinds of covert activity done in the name of national security since 1947 have not only compromised the integrity of the Oval Office, but have also compromised the notion of freedom, both here at home and around the world. Under the national security state, the voice of the masses is too often silenced. Instead, the will of those who control national security policy is carried out under an overly authoritarian kind of methodology.

In his book, Brave New World Order, Jack Nelson-Pallmeyer identified seven characteristics of a national security state.

> The first characteristic of a National Security State is that the military is the highest authority. In a National Security State, the military not only guarantees the security of the state against all internal and external enemies, it has enough power to determine the overall direction of the society. In a National Security State, the military exerts important influence over political, economic, as well as military affairs. A second defining feature of a National Security State is that political democracy and democratic elections are viewed with suspicion, contempt, or in terms of political expediency. National Security States often maintain an appearance of democracy. However, ultimate power rests with the military or within a broader National Security Establishment. A third characteristic of a National Security State

is that the military and related sectors wield substantial political and economic power. They do so in the context of an ideology which stresses that "freedom" and "development" are possible only when capital is concentrated in the hands of elite. A fourth feature of a National Security State is its obsession with enemies. There are enemies of the state everywhere. Defending against external and/or internal enemies becomes a leading preoccupation of the state, a distorting factor in the economy, and a major source of national identity and purpose. A fifth ideological foundation of a National Security State is that the enemies of the state are cunning and ruthless. Therefore, any means used to destroy or control these enemies is justified. A sixth characteristic of a National Security State is that it restricts public debate and limits popular participation through secrecy or intimidation. Authentic democracy depends on participation of the people. National Security States limit such participation in a number of ways: They sow fear and thereby narrow the range of public debate; they restrict and distort information; and they define policies in secret and implement those policies through covert channels and clandestine activities. The state justifies such actions through rhetorical pleas of "higher purpose" and vague appeals to "national security." Finally, the church is expected to mobilize its financial, ideological, and theological resources in service to the National Security State (Nelson-Pallmeyer 1992).

In Bill Moyer's PBS documentary, "The Secret Government," Admiral Gene Le Roque, a former strategic planner for the Pentagon, bravely tells us the history, the scope, and the compromises to our domestic tranquility under the national security state.

> Now, that National Security Act of 1947 changed dramatically the direction of this great nation. It established the framework for a national security state. The National Security Act of '47 gave us the National Security Council. Never have we had a National Security Council so concerned about the nation's security that we are always looking for threats and looking how to orchestrate our society to oppose those threats. National Security was invented, almost, in 1947, and now it has become the prime mover of everything we do, and is measured against something we invented in 1947 (Moyers 1987).

The Reorganization of Intelligence

The National Security Act of 1947 brought about an almost total reorganization of the foreign policy and military infrastructure of the United States. The Act established many useful institutions critical to the changes in U.S. foreign policy in the post-Cold War world for American presidents. Some of the organizations are the National Security Council (NSC), which included the President, Vice President, Secretary of State, Secretary of Defense, and the Director of the CIA. The Council meets at the White House to discuss both long- and short-term national security issues. The President's Assistant for National Security Affairs directs a small NSC staff that coordinates materials from other agencies for the President's consideration on matters of foreign policy. Each President has wide latitude to use the power of the NSC the way he chooses. Different levels and degrees of importance, autonomy, and influence over all other government agencies are given to the NSC staff.

The National Security Act of 1947 abolished the Office of Strategic Services (OSS), which served America's intelligence gathering functions during World War II. Filling the intelligence gap created by dissolving the OSS, the Central Intelligence Agency (CIA) was created under the National Security Act. Since then, intelligence gathering has been divided between two agencies: The CIA has conducted most civilian intelligence gathering, and the Defense Intelligence Agency became the main source for military intelligence gathering.

The National Security Act of 1947 also brought about seismic changes in the structure of America's military. The War Department and Navy Department were abolished. The combined functions of both organizations were consolidated into the Department of Defense (DOD). Operating from the Pentagon, the Secretary of Defense is in charge of both the DOD and the Department of the Air Force. All of the three branches of the military, the Air Force, Army, and Navy, each operate under their own Secretaries, who, since 1949, in turn, operate under the Secretary of Defense.

Presidents Truman, Eisenhower, Kennedy, Johnson, and Nixon

Members of the Council on Foreign Relations, who also dominated the State Department, also dominated the NSC during the Truman years and continue to do so today. The NSC directed most of America's foreign policy during the Eisenhower administration, but it took a backseat to different executive committees of trusted advisors during the Kennedy and Johnson administrations. Henry A. Kissinger headed President Nixon's NSC staff and used the NSC to negotiate with foreign leaders and advance the foreign policy objectives of Nixon and Kissinger.

President Carter

Under the Carter presidency, the National Security Advisor was Dr. Zbigniew Brzezinski. Dr. Brzezinski became the principal official that the President relied upon for foreign policy.

Dr. Brzezinski, in my opinion, is probably the best National Security Advisor in the history of the NSC. I'll take just a moment to explain my assessment. I've had the opportunity to interview Dr. Brzezinski on the radio, and as I told him, I believe that he, not President Reagan, was probably the most influential individual in the American government in defeating the Soviet Union and bringing the perilous and costly Cold War to an end. His actions today are the subject of controversy, but at the time, they were justified because they were carried out to neutralize a truly critical threat to

America's national security, not the kind of murky agenda we currently find underway in Iraq. Dr. Brzezinski faced the threats posed by the Soviets pragmatically and was motivated to protect the world from the unthinkable. As far as I'm concerned, the big red dog was a far greater threat to our liberty than Saddam ever was. I, for one, am grateful that Dr. Brzezinski's efforts were successful.

The actions of Dr. Brzezinski brought about a conclusion to the most dangerous conflict mankind has ever seen, and it was done without directly shedding American blood. However, setting the stage for the Soviet Union's collapse in their war with Afghanistan was risky and ultimately strengthened groups that would later become terrorists against the West. While I am sensitive to all the issues of human rights and governmental sovereignty that Tariq Ali talks about in his book, The Clash of Fundamentalisms: Crusades, Jihads, and Modernity, I must conclude that when one considers the alternatives to ending the tenuous conflict in relations between the two great superpowers, a conflict described by Khrushchev as nearly irresolvable without thermonuclear war, it may have been the only way out. During the Cuban Missile Crisis, which was the most dangerous period of the Cold War, Khrushchev said,

> Mr. President, we and you ought not now to pull on the ends of the rope in which you have tied the knot of war, because the more the two of us pull, the tighter that knot will be tied. And a moment may come when that knot will be tied so tight that even he who tied it will not have the strength to untie it, and then it will be necessary

to cut that knot, and what that would mean is
not for me to explain to you, because you yourself
understand perfectly of what terrible forces our
countries possess. Consequently, if there is not
intention to tighten that knot and thereby doom
the world to the catastrophe of thermonuclear
war, then let us not only relax the forces pulling
on the ends of the rope, let us take measures to
untie the knot. We are ready for this (Tariq Ali
2003).

The potential for the U.S. and the U.S.S.R. to destroy
all life on this planet was — and still is — real. I'm just glad
that tensions have significantly been reduced and
brinkmanship with nukes is no longer a constant element of
our lives.

President Reagan

We have already discussed, in overview, the way covert
and illegal policies of the Reagan White House violated the
Constitution, the will of Congress, and the will of the
American people in the name of national security. We will
return to this story later. For now, suffice it to say that the so-
called collegial approach to foreign policy decision-making
being emphasized in the Reagan administration was
problematic enough to allow Iran/Contra to materialize.
Conflicts arose which became public as the NSC staff
operated as a separate and contending entity within the
government.

Under Reagan, the NSC became a shadow
government within the government. Subsequently, President

Reagan, Vice-President George Herbert Walker Bush, Defense Secretary Weinberger, and others within the administration denied knowledge of the illegal sales of arms to Iran to fund and support the Contra's war efforts. This denial was contrary to the ultimate findings of independent prosecutor Lawrence Walsh, who determined that the President probably did know about it.

National Security Advisor John Poindexter was convicted of conspiracy to obstruct inquiries and proceedings, issuing false statements, falsification, destruction and removal of documents, obstruction of Congress, and two counts of false statements. This conviction was overturned by a technicality. Poindexter's lawyers were relying on the issue of their client's immunized testimony being allegedly used against him to get him off. It was the only card they could play, and it worked. Poindexter walked.

President George H.W. Bush

During the presidency of George Herbert Walker Bush, the national security monster was forced into collegiality. We did not see quite the level of shananigans under Bush as we saw under his predecessor, Reagan. Nevertheless, there are a few points concerning G.H.W. Bush's foreign policy that were, and still, remain questionable. Granted, he achieved his stated objectives of liberating Kuwait and forcing Iraqi withdrawal after Saddam Hussein's invasion, but I personally question why Saddam was given the tacit nod on his invasion in the first place. According to the Christian Science Monitor, May 27, 1999, U.S. Ambassador Glaspie had "in effect given Saddam a green light to invade Kuwait" (Cole 1999). There are many people in America who also question why Bush then called off combat operations, effectively letting Saddam Hussein stay in power.

But therein lies the area where the actions of President George Herbert Walker Bush's NSC make those of his son appear all the more puzzling. What do I mean? It's amazing to see how the worm turns, because G.H.W. Bush's Secretary of Defense, Dick Cheney, warned that invading Iraq at that juncture would cause the United States to get "bogged down in the quagmire inside Iraq" (Cole 1999).

Today, the same Dick Cheney is now Vice President under G.H.W. Bush's son, President George W. Bush, and their administration has done just that — unilaterally invaded Iraq. Today, many people believe that the U.S. is, in fact, "bogged down in the quagmire in Iraq." Likewise, G.H.W. Bush's explanation for not moving toward regime change and, thereby, occupying Iraq because of the "incalculable human and political costs" is equally opposite to the current policy of his son's administration, which is of regime change and occupation.

G.H.W. Bush's explanation for not removing Saddam Hussein made sense. The Gulf War soldiers, he said, "whose life would be on my hands as the commander in chief because I, unilaterally, went beyond the international law, went beyond the stated mission and said we're going to show our macho. We're going into Baghdad. We're going to be an occupying power — America in an Arab land — with no allies at our side. It would have been disastrous" (Cole 1999).

President Clinton

President Clinton even further expanded the structural scope of the NSC, but did not neglect to create a more egalitarian NSC within the jurisdiction of the Constitution. Under Clinton, a more pragmatic regard for a coalition of our allies was held than we see today. Clinton also delegated power on matters of national security within the NSC with the kind of transparency and accountability that the Reagan/Bush or the G.W. Bush administrations would not. Under Clinton, the Secretary of the Treasury, the U.S. Representative to the United Nations, and the Assistant to the President for Economic Policy, along with the National Economic Council (NEC), the President's Chief of Staff, and the President's National Security Adviser, were all added to the NSC.

President George W. Bush

On September 20, 2002, President George W. Bush unveiled his new strategy on America's national security. This new policy constituted a doctrinal shift that eradicated the doctrine of deterrence, which sustained the peace during the Cold War years. Instead, Bush opted for a radical new strategic policy unlike anything America has ever seen.

Under this administration, America has now embarked upon a strategic policy of unilateral preemption against hostile states and terrorist groups. In other words, Bush has chosen to attack his potential enemies before they attack America or its interests.

Under his alleged policy of expanding development assistance and expanding free trade, more jobs have been outsourced, and there is a growing trade deficit. These negative by-products now threaten to become permanent fixtures. What this means is that America is now engaged in perpetual war at a time of unprecedented expanding economic hardship — without an end in sight.

I also question the logistics of Bush's policy of promoting democracy in the Middle East. These are states which, throughout the recorded history of their cultures, have never demonstrated a propensity toward an American-style democratic political ideology. I believe that the structural social, economic, and political impediments to the development of democracy in the Middle East, which are many, are being grossly underestimated by the Bush administration. Most states in the Middle East are notoriously nationalistic, rife with cronyism and corruption, and they bristle at outside intervention, particularly from the West.

Likewise, forcing democracy upon those people, while at the same time fighting a very resilient insurgency with an overextended military and rebuilding the political, economic, and industrial infrastructure of Iraq, is an incommensurable challenge, not to mention the political stakes at risk for the 2006 midterm elections. Republicans are shaking in their boots as the public grows weary of dealing with a scandal-ridden foreign policy quagmire and its highly probable failure.

When this nation chooses such a tenuous objective as democratization of the Middle East, it makes it even more difficult to fulfill its commitment to fighting disease and fostering economic development, which are central pillars of the National Security Act of 1947. The Bush administration has a poor record in all these areas.

Chapter Two

★ ★ ★ ★ ★

20th Century U.S. Presidential Policies on Strategic Petroleum Reserves

How the United States government organizes foreign policy and deals with its national security concerns in the 21st century can not be fully understood outside of the historical progression of America's strategic relationship to oil markets. Briefly, this is a saga of Anglo-American domination of oil production in the early 20th century transmuting into a bloody and economically asphyxiating level of U.S. petroleum dependence in the latter half of the 20th century.

Too many of us have forgotten, or never knew, that America used to be the world's leading producer and supplier of oil, as well as many other commodities that once made this nation's economic foundation solid and robust. In other words, some of us are simply clueless about why and how this transformation of official U.S. policy on strategic petroleum came about. So we labor upon this treadmill of our petroleum-based economy, working harder and harder each year, thoroughly perplexed and full of anxiety about our future. The working class in this nation has yet to become fully aware of how and why we've lost our economic compass and flounder in this dispensation, dangerously close to history's rocky heap of deceased empires. A clear and complete mental image of how this happened cannot be fully formed until all the pieces of the puzzle are in place.

For most of us, a major piece of the puzzle is still missing, without which, again, it is almost impossible to frame a clear perspective. Our international strategic predicament, our economic peril, and our worldview must be framed within the context of our petroleum policy as it relates to the rise of the National Security State.

Over the last 60 years, since the passage of the National Security Act of 1947, we have gone from a production economy to a service economy to what is now a multiple asset bubble economy. The thrust of this degeneration has been fueled in part by 20th century presidential policies on strategic petroleum reserves. America's attempts to spread its hegemony and too often unilaterally lead, shape, and mold a new world order during this period, have sadly contributed significantly to the increased level of avarice and confrontations in the world. In effect, as Lenin said, we indeed "labor in preparation for our own suicide" (Richman 1985).

Most Americans are unaware of the fact that some of America's oil companies actually supplied oil for our enemies during times of war in the 20th century. This is well documented by Charles Higham in Trading with the Enemy: The Nazi American Money Plot 1933–1945. Therefore, advancing U.S. presidential policies on strategic petroleum reserves has always been both costly and dangerous. In this process, we've not only robbed ourselves to feed our glut for oil, but we've actually become less secure in the process.

The Roosevelt Doctrine

In an effort to meet the expanding world demand for petroleum, one of the highest strategic countermeasures to Soviet expansionism in the second half of the 20th century has been maintaining Western domination of world oil production. Upon the prospect of compromising U.S. oil reserves while advancing this strategic mandate in dealing with the Soviet Union, President Franklin Roosevelt worked to establish surrogate oil production. In other words, Roosevelt realized that U.S. oil reserves are finite, and America shouldn't deplete its reserves while facing Soviet competition for global hegemony. This led to a marriage of both convenience and strategic necessity between the United States and the House of Saud.

In short, during February of 1945, Roosevelt cut a deal with King Abdul Aziz bin Saud aboard the USS Quincy in the Nile Canal. The deal called for Saudi Arabia's oil in exchange for the U.S. providing protection from Saudi Arabia's enemies in the Middle East. Because the fundamentalist regimes surrounding Saudi Arabia would eventually become resentful of Saudi dibbling and dabbling with the West, this was a meeting that would forever change U.S. geo-strategic policy in the Middle East. America needed their oil, and the U.S. government was willing to tackle the added risks and expense to acquire it. So, in spite of the prospects of a pro-Western Saudi regime becoming a source of strife and instability in the Middle East, from that day forward, America was joined at the hip to the chaos and volatility of the Middle East. It didn't matter if this move would increase tension in the desert; America had one-upped the Soviet Union, who also wanted to control the resources of the region. True to Roosevelt's pledge, America successfully obstructed the Soviet Union and all others who have sought to gain control of not only the Saudi oil reserves, but also the entire Persian Gulf region.

The Truman Doctrine

The Truman Doctrine, in a nutshell, further advanced the policy of America protecting free nations from the threat of Soviet expansionism. To accomplish that goal, the Truman agenda had to be based on a dominating Anglo-American access and influence on Middle East oil reserves.

As I've said, after World War II, there was a seismic shift in strategic petroleum policy in the U.S., and the center of world oil production moved from America to the Middle East. In the beginning of this period, Britain controlled four-fifths of that output. But after the end of the Truman administration in 1953, the British lost most of its share, dropping to 31 percent. Simultaneously, the U.S. share had risen to 60 percent. This dramatic change is a direct result of

President Harry Truman's policy on strategic petroleum reserves. Truman was determined to advance Anglo-American hegemony, and controlling the resources of the Persian Gulf region was the key. So Truman commissioned a committee of bankers and businessmen, led by Chase National Bank President Winthrop Aldrich (brother-in-law of John D. Rockefeller), to, among other things, enlarge the Anglo-American share of oil production. This was the basis of the Truman Doctrine. It should also be noted that the Marshall Plan was also a major part of this overall strategy.

Much of the Marshall Plan's aid to Europe between 1948 and 1952 was spent in a way that prioritized the interests of the Anglo-American oil trust. Contrary to popular perception in America, Marshall Plan funds were not only used to rebuild infrastructure like streets, bridges, and buildings destroyed in bombings during World War II in Europe, but were heavily funneled into the coffers of Standard Oil of New York and Standard Oil of New Jersey. Major British refineries were constructed with the Marshall Plan's aid to Europe after World War II.

Thus, the Marshall Plan was very useful in compromising the free market by undercutting independent U.S. refineries in the European market. Additionally, the U.S. government bought Middle East oil, which then cost 50 cents a barrel to produce, from these quasi-proxy firms at the Texas Gulf Coast price of $2.65, further increasing profits for the oil trust under the guise of rectifying Allied damage to other infrastructures in post-war Europe. Most revealing is this statement from Walter Levy, who left Standard Oil of New York to head the Marshall Plan's oil division,

Without the Marshall Plan, the American oil business in Europe would already have been shot to pieces ... Without Marshall Plan aid, Europe would have not been able to afford during the last year, and could not afford during the next three years, to import large quantities of American oil — from either domestic or foreign sources controlled by American companies ... The Plan does not believe that Europe should save dollars or earn foreign exchange by driving American oil from the European market (Liggio1979).

In fulfilling presidential policies on strategic petroleum reserves, Middle East oil has become the most expensive in the world market today. This is because of the astronomical level of taxpayer money that is spent on a defense model designed not to protect the U.S. from tactical military threats, but largely to protect Anglo-American oil infrastructure and its interests in the Middle East. Consideration should also be given to the number of young American lives which have been sacrificed for these goals when calculating the total costs for our crackhead-like addiction to Middle East oil.

U.S. Doctrine and the Rise of OPEC

To understand the basics of the Eisenhower Doctrine on strategic petroleum reserves, read the chapter on Operation Ajax. U.S. presidential policies on strategic petroleum reserves remained largely unaltered through the Kennedy and Johnson years as America was focused on protecting its hegemony by facing the Soviet proxy force in

Southeast Asia during the Vietnam War. During that period, beginning in the early 1970s, the honeymoon of the Anglo-American petroleum establishment's clandestine marriage with the Saudis began to sour.

The Saudi kingdom's vast oil reserves and their fortuitous willingness to use its unequalled production capacity to support, moderate, and stabilize oil prices on the world market were vital to American's petroleum industrialists and its national security as well. These were the days, before the existence of the Organization of Petroleum Exporting Countries (OPEC), when the powerful oil cartels of the West often retained 65 percent or more of the revenue from a product that was produced on someone else's property.

America realized the strategic advantage of domestic petroleum conservation through proxy production accords. Saman Sapheri's article in the International Socialist Review, entitled, "The Geopolitics of Oil," tells us that today, OPEC's membership includes "Saudi Arabia, Algeria, Indonesia, Iran, Iraq, Kuwait, Libya, Nigeria, Qatar, United Arab Emirates, and Venezuela" (Sapheri 2002). For economic and strategic purposes, occasionally, Canada, Mexico, Norway, Russia, and other oil-producing nations outside OPEC will sometimes go along with the cartel's accords.

The reason for establishing OPEC was to create a unified front for greater leverage against the West's oil cartels. Having learned the lessons about how "competition is sin" from John D. Rockefeller and J.P. Morgan, the giant oil cartels of the West were working closely together. The oil-producing nations hoped the creation of OPEC would allow the producer nations to establish a counterbalance and eventually nationalize petroleum production, thereby seizing much more revenue from their resources.

In spite of its confrontational hegemonic agenda, OPEC remained benign from its founding in 1960 until 1973. It was in that year that all hell broke loose. As I have said, OPEC was the primary vehicle used in pursuing the economic interests of America's proxy oil suppliers. By taking the lead in establishing OPEC, the Saudi royals became enticed by the position of being the principal beneficiary of a unified challenge to U.S. hegemony and began to tactically renege on their 1945 deal with the Roosevelt administration.

On the Jewish holy day of Yom Kippur, October 6, 1973, Egyptian forces attacked Israel from across the Suez Canal. Simultaneously, in a surprise offensive, Syria attacked the Golan Heights. Israel quickly pushed Syria back into the northern territory and outflanked the Egyptian army in the south. With help from the U.S., Israel reversed the Arab insurgency, and the killing ended in November.

Because American involvement in the conflict enabled Israel's success, Saudi Arabia felt that the U.S. did not honor its Roosevelt Doctrine, and on October 17, OPEC struck back. This time, their target was the United States and her European allies. Their tactical response was an oil embargo on the U.S., and a simultaneous increase in oil prices to the tune of 70 percent for America's allies in Europe.

By January 1974, the price of a barrel of OPEC crude had risen from $3 to $11.65. In addition, OPEC was able to take advantage of a fortuitous opportunity and added an exclamation point upon the U.S. and the Netherlands for their support of Israel in the war. In October of that same year, during an environment of elevated tensions between the U.S. and Soviet Union who were conducting naval operations in the Mediterranean, OPEC disregarded the spirit of the Roosevelt agreement with the Saudis and cut off oil supplies to the U.S. Navy.

The early 1970s was a very volatile period. The industrialized world was experiencing unprecedented inflationary expansion. The free world was exposed to tremendous risk because of the domination of oil and other commodity cartels. Two decades of profound growth and advancement of the industrial world created heavy demand for oil, as well as for most other raw materials.

The U.S. Department of Commerce found that consumer prices were rising at a rate of 8.5 percent. Inflation rates in other nations were dragging their economies like a kayak trying to tow a nuclear aircraft carrier. The demand for proxy oil supplies, particularly in the Middle East, was at an all-time high. The demand for oil in the industrialized world far outpaced all surrogate production capabilities. For America's national security concerns, OPEC's attempt to gain strategic leverage was reaching a critical mass with no sign of slowing. For the West's oil cartels, OPEC's demand for a greater share of the profits was a major problem.

By 1973, facing increasing stress on domestic reserves, America was importing 35 percent of its oil. In March of that year, President Nixon began experimenting with petroleum price controls. What would happen next would send the markets reeling. Oil stocks were buoyed by rising profits as speculators indulged exuberantly.

But the Dow Jones industrial average fell from 962 to 822. The entire Western world was going through a nasty recession. Motorists lined up for gasoline in cars that stretched for blocks. The hardship of the increase from 30 cents to about $1.20 per gallon was making the consumer livid. On March 18, 1974, with the Dow at 874 and global equity markets in a tizzy, OPEC lifted its damaging embargo against the U.S.

Many people believed the whole crisis was being intentionally created and perpetuated by "big oil," plundering the little guy for profits. But in reality, it was public indifference and ignorance of U.S. presidential policies on strategic petroleum reserves that allowed our leaders to create the kind of geo-political confrontations that elicit these kinds of tactical responses from our enemies upon the unwitting American consumer. Since that time, the rationale for this quid pro quo arrangement with the Saudi royals has been questioned, particularly in the liberal circles of the think tanks and NGOs in the West. People began questioning whether or not the advantages of Saudi dependence were outweighed by disadvantages. But that questioning was not confined to the West.

By 1979, revolution was underway in Iran when, as feared by Roosevelt and the Saudi royal family, Iranian clerics began to challenge the religious credentials of the Saudi monarchy because of their experiments with cultural westernization. It is this kind of environment of political and economic instability in the Middle East, brought on by internal tribalism, religious conflict, war, Western-inspired coups, and resource privatization that forms the perfect breeding ground for despotic leaders to rise to power.

The establishment of the anti-American and anti-Saudi "Islamic Republic" in Tehran with its new leader, the Ayatollah Khomeini, condemning Saudi royals as radically secular and corrupt was a natural outgrowth of diplomacy by deception on all sides.

In the final analysis, given the key role of oil to economic growth, America's oil dependency and the geopolitical and strategic complications associated with U.S. presidential policies on strategic petroleum reserves has been, and still is, one of the prime causes of our economic and strategic vulnerability. The sooner America rids itself of the petroleum-based economy, the better her national security will be.

Chapter Three

★ ★ ★ ★ ★

The Rise of the Cold War

Operation Paperclip

The aim here is to begin to give the reader a brief overview of the kinds of covert operations that have become a part of the national security state. First we will look at project called "Operation Paperclip" (originally called Operation Overcast). The events that took place during Operation Paperclip, and throughout the period discussed here, marked the first major doctrinal shift in intelligence gathering after the defeat of Nazi forces in the late 1940s. From that time on, the United States officially began to profoundly expand upon the policy of relying upon covert industrial and corporate espionage without aversion to involvement with even the most despotic sources. In other words, U.S. intelligence officials no longer cared about the evil done by their foreign intelligence assets, and as long as they could be of help in the Cold War, their crimes would be overlooked, and sometimes, as in the case of Operation Paperclip, covered up.

After World War II, the seeds of global change began to germinate. The old strategic relationships and alliances that existed during the war had changed, and a Cold War had begun. In other words, the former friends of America became America's enemies. Whereas Russia was our ally during World War II against the Germans and the Japanese, they were now America's enemy, and Germany and Japan became America's friends. Therefore, since the world had undergone a historic strategic realignment, the political and military scientists in the U.S. decided it necessitated America realigning its military, foreign policy, and its entire intelligence apparatus. The National Security Act, along with the Truman Doctrine and the Marshall Plan, were major components of the Truman administration's Cold War strategic policy of "containment."

Winston Churchill said, "An Iron Curtain has descended the continent. Behind that line lay all the capitals of the ancient states of Eastern and Central Europe" (Mackler 2005). As I have said, during World War II, before that Iron Curtain descended across Europe, the Soviet Union was America's ally. By the end of the war, they were America's enemy and the U.S. government would stop at nothing to prevent them from achieving a dominant enough position to force upon mankind their version of a New World Order. We were even willing to overlook the crimes perpetrated by the Nazis or any of our former enemies and begin working with them to defeat the Communists.

Both America and the Soviet Union were feverishly engaged in plundering Germany. Both sides wanted strategic advantages. Therefore, the engineers and intelligence officers of the Nazi war machine became the most coveted spoils of the war. Whoever laid claim to their talents would hold significant advantages in the development of aerospace technology, as well as in nuclear, chemical, and biological weapons development. The only problem for the U.S. government lay in the fact that it was illegal for war criminals to immigrate to the United States, and that's what many of these former Nazis were. So in September 1946, Truman agreed to authorize a covert plan called Operation Paperclip, which allowed the OSS to bring in these former German scientists and intelligence officials to aid in America's efforts against its new enemy, the Soviet Union.

President Truman fully realized the disastrous political ramifications of a government-inspired breach of our immigration law, especially with regard to some of Hitler's henchmen. Truman did not want to allow anyone found, in his words, "to have been a member of the Nazi party and more than a nominal participant in its activities, or an active supporter of Naziism or militarism" (Mackler 2005) to immigrate to America. The job of separating the good Nazis from the bad Nazis was assigned to the War Department's Joint Intelligence Objectives Agency (JIOA).

In the early part of 1947, the JIOA concluded what can initially be described as a set of damning background investigations of Hitler's former scientists. When the director of the JIOA, Bosquet Wev, submitted the first set of scientists' dossiers to the State and Justice departments for review,

Samauel Klaus, the representative of the State Department on the JIOA board, claimed that all the scientists in this first batch were "ardent Nazis"(Mackler 2005) and turned down their visa requests. This was not the outcome that the JIOA was looking for. Many people in the corporate military industrial establishment wouldn't be happy if they could not have full advantage in the development of new military technologies. These Nazi "smart boys" were the key in assuring America's strategic and finanical advantage in the Cold War.

I do believe President Truman primarily sought strategic advantage for the safety of our citizens. But that doesn't negate the fact that powerful banking and corporate interests heavily influenced policies of the newly created NSC for the purpose of assuring Western global economic hegemony without the complications of due process. In other words, the government had its agenda, which was largely strategic, and the financial and industrial establishment had theirs, which was primarily monetary. Both were seeking to be served through the policies of the NSC. Consider, for example, the amount of money that Lockheed is now making off of America's national, security-related spending. According to an article by Jack Mackler entitled "Lockheed, the King of Warfare,"

> Remember the term "military-industrial complex?" It used to conjure up images of an array of U.S. corporations that produced weapons of war for super-profits. President Dwight D. Eisenhower warned against these military contractors exercising undue influence over government. In the 1970s, the Lockheed

Corporation was one of several in this field. Remember some of the others? Martin Marietta, General Electric Aerospace, Goodyear Aerospace, RCA, General Dynamics/Fort Worth, General Dynamics Space Systems, Honeywell EO, LTV Missiles, IBM Federal Systems, Unisys Defense, Ford Aerospace, Xerox Electro-Optical Systems, Gould Ocean Systems, Libra-scope, Sanders, OAO, and Fairchild Weston? They're all gone today, merged or acquired by one mega-corporation, the king of weapons manufacturing and all associated technologies, Lockheed Martin (Weiner 2004).

Each year, Mackler adds, "Lockheed's sales will likely increase in a nation where national security spending exceeds a half-trillion dollars annually." New York Times staff writer Tim Weiner's Nov. 28, 2004, article, "Lockheed and the Future of Warfare," offers a rare peek into an industry and corporation that epitomizes the relationship between capitalism's private property interests and the strategic interests of government. He said,

> Obviously, war and crisis have been good for business. The Pentagon's budget for buying new weapons rose by about a third over the last three years, to $81 billion in fiscal 2004, up from $60 billion in 2001. Lockheed's sales also rose by about a third, to nearly $32 billion in the 2003 calendar year, from $24 billion in 2001. It was the No. 1 recipient of Pentagon primary contracts, with $21.9 billion in fiscal 2003. Boeing had $17.3 billion, Northrop Grumman had $11.1 billion and

General Dynamics had $8.2 billion (Weiner 2004).

The aim here is not to beat up on Lockheed, but to illustrate how the actions and directives of the NSC assure amazing amounts of money for corporate and industrial interests in the name of national security. During the Operation Paperclip period, the tremendous amount of money that the Anglo-American banking and corporate establishments stood to lose in not being able to finance the development of these new technologies and other global industrial developments as well was staggering. Great pressure was put on the JIOA to resolve this sticky situation. Too much money was at stake to allow something as silly as patriotism, nationalism, and justice to stand in the way. Besides, remember the attitude of those who sought to use the NSC's power to ensure their profits was such that it didn't matter if these German scientists were criminals; after all, we weren't at war with Germany anymore anyway.

In a book by Carol Rutz called A Nation Betrayed, she chronicles the activities of the U.S. intelligence community in this area. She tells us how the U.S. was willing to forget about former war criminals and not allow anything to threaten the success of their operations. She reveals the desperate attitudes of the U.S. intelligence apparatus, working diligently to accomplish their goal of reaping the spoils of Nazi Germany.

This was echoed by JIOA's Director Bosquet Wev in a frantic and angry memo warning that "the best interests of the United States have been subjugated to the efforts expended in beating a dead Nazi horse" (Rutz 2005). She went on to warn that we could not return these scientists to Germany, where they could be harnessed by America's enemies. These assets were regarded as indispensable, and losing them to the Soviets presented a "far greater security threat to this country than any former Nazi affiliations which they may have had or even any Nazi sympathies that they may still have" (Rutz 2005). Rutz also records a wire sent to the director of intelligence at the U.S. European Command.

> There is very little possibility that the State and Justice Departments will agree to immigrate any specialist who has been classified as an actual or potential security threat to the United States. This may result in the return to Germany of specialists whose skill and knowledge should be denied to other nations in the interest of national security. He then requested, "... THAT NEW SECURITY REPORTS BE SUBMITTED WHERE SUCH ACTION IS APPROPRIATE" [emphasis added] (Rutz 2005).

> In other words, cover up the bad stuff.

The mandate was clear, but the task was politically delicate. If the American people ever fully understood that their loved ones died fighting the very men who were now heading much of America's post-war weapons development and aerospace programs, particularly so soon after the war, they might not approve. This was an operation that had to be conducted in total secrecy, and failure was not an option.

That's why immediately after the JIOA was created, it began the work of recruiting the Nazi smart boys. The director of what would become the Central Intelligence

Agency, Allen Dulles, sat down for a "meeting of the minds" with the powerful Nazi intelligence leader in Germany, Reinhard Gehlen. Dulles and Gehlen were birds of a feather, so they understood each other. The two men were able to form a relationship at the very first meeting, which assured American control of one of the most powerful transnational intelligence assets in the Cold War era.

The knowledge Gehlen gained as a master spy for the Nazis, having infiltrated Russia with his large Nazi intelligence network, was invaluable to America's strategic interests. It was of the utmost importance for Dulles to make Gehlen and his vast intelligence unit a safe and influential asset in the American intelligence establishment.

Sidestepping the entire problem of Gehlen's war crimes, American intelligence specialists rewrote the scientist's dossier, eliminating incriminating evidence and delivering the Nazi intelligence specialist and much of his network to the United States instead of to the war tribunals at Nuremberg. What would follow would be a host of covert umbrella projects in the area of areospace, chemical, and biological weapons development — all the result of a secret continuation of research from Hitler's Nazi scientists.

Following are some of the Nazi war criminals who escaped Nuremberg to have their files sanitized and were put to work for the United States under the Office of Strategic Service's Operation Paperclip:

- **Wernher Van Braun:** He developed the V2 rocket that devastated the Allies during World War II. Arriving in the U.S. on September 29, 1945, Van

Braun was among the first group of German scientists to be put to work at Fort Strong, Boston. About 130 German scientists and technical personnel had signed temporary work contracts with the Army at the close of World War II. Then, in the mid-40s, a decision was made to station the German scientists at Fort Bliss, Texas, where an Army guided missile proving ground was established. Van Braun worked on guided missiles for the Army, and later became the head of NASA and developed the Saturn 5 rocket used in the Apollo program.

- **Heinrich Rupp:** Rupp was convicted of bank fraud during the 1980s savings and loan debacle. He, along with former CIA chief William Casey, who was then campaign manager for Ronald Reagan, flew with George H.W. Bush to Paris in 1980. In his subsequent testimony before a Federal Jury, he stated that three meetings were held there from October 19–20. The subject of those meetings was the sabotage of Jimmy Carter's reelection by delaying the release of the hostages. The hostages were released on January 20, 1981, immediately after Reagan and Bush were sworn into office. The Reagan administration then released Iran's frozen assets in the United States, enabling the Iranians to illegally purchase arms from America in what would become known as the Iran/Contra Affair.

- **Klaus Barbie:** Known as the butcher of Lyons, France, during World War II, Barbie was responsible for the torture and mass murder of thousands of Allied civilians under German occupation in France. In a 1987 PBS documentary by Bill Moyers entitled, "The Secret Government," Erhard Dabringhaus, a U.S. Army Intelligence official who worked with Nazi informants as spies against the U.S.S.R., tells us that one of the spies that he worked with was Klaus Barbie himself:

"One that I know real well is Klaus Barbie. He was wanted by the French as their number one war criminal. And, somehow, we employed a man like that as a very secretive informant. During the time I learned that Barbie was really such a brutal murderer, I reported this to my headquarters and I thought I was going to get a promotion. I thought there was a big picture of a deal in here. And the answer was — Dabringhaus, keep quiet until he's no longer useful then we'll turn him over to the French. Under those conditions, I thought, OK, let's work with him. As an intelligence officer, you work with the devil" (Moyers 1987).

- **Kurt Blome:** One of the highest-ranking Nazi scientists in Germany who, under interrogation by the U.S. military in 1945, revealed that in 1943, he performed experiments on concentration camp prisoners with plague vaccines. He was tried and acquitted at Nuremberg in 1947 for systematically exterminating sick prisoners and conducting experiments on humans. Two months after his Nuremberg acquittal, because of his expertise in chemo/bio warfare, Blome was brought to Camp David, Maryland, and in 1951, he was hired by the U.S. Army Chemical Corps to work on chemical warfare. Nothing about his

Nuremberg trial was allowed to be written in his JIOA file.

- **Authur Rudolph:** A member of the Nazi party since 1931. According to his 1945 military file, he was "100% Nazi, dangerous type, security threat! Suggest internment" (Lasby 1975). During the war, Rudolph ran the Mittelwerk factory at the Dora-Nordhausen concentration camps. Under his watch, 20,000 workers died from various forms of inhumane torture and physical abuse. The JIOA sanitized his final dossier, saying that there was "nothing in his records indicating that he was a war criminal or an ardent Nazi or otherwise objectionable" (Lasby 1975). Rudolph received his U.S. citizenship, and along with Van Braun, went on to work on the Saturn 5 rocket used in the Apollo program.

These are just a few of the over 700 dubious individuals brought into this country under Operation Paperclip. Yes, I know it is shocking to find out that after World War II, the United States employed the use of Nazi war criminals in the establishment of various aspects of the American national security state apparatus. Nevertheless, it is true. Nazis were put to work in our military intelligence establishment, our chemical and biological weapons program, our nuclear weapons program, in the medical establishment, in education, and even in the space program.

But this wasn't really the beginning of the West's covert, friendly relationship with the Nazi elite. We were simply helping those who were helped all along by American and British corporate interests during the war.

In a book called Trading with the Enemy: The Nazi American Money Plot 1933–1949, Higham reveals the fact that just as Allied forces were told to stand down and allow the refueling of Hitler's warships by Standard Oil of New Jersey to take place, the hands-off policy for these criminals continued after the war.

As Erhard Dabringhaus found out, the orchestrators of Operation Paperclip were insistent upon making friends with these former notorious enemies of America: "They seemed to have had a preconceived program of what the Communists are up to. And if I sent in a report that there was a Nazi war criminal running around over there, forget it; we're not interested in the Nazis anymore. We're concentrating on the Communists" (Moyers 1987).

Chapter Four

★ ★ ★ ★ ★

Operation Ajax
The Lessons of 1953

With this basic understanding of what took place under Operation Paperclip, it is now time to reexamine another example of right-wing abuse of power under the national security state apparatus. In what can only be described as a seminal event in the modern history of the Middle East, the United States and Great Britain initiated a joint, covert regime change operation called "Operation Ajax" in Iran during 1953. This holds important lessons for today.

This chapter will shed vital new light on issues that remain crucial to the evolution of relations between the United States and the so-called Axis of Evil: Iraq, Iran, and North Korea. It is my hope that more Americans will continue to question the ramifications of covert operations, preemption, and unilateralism in U.S. foreign policy.

The overthrow of the democratically elected Muhammad Mossadeq and his government in Iran is a prime example of the subversion of those democratic ideals for which America is supposed to stand. Rather than honesty, statesmanship, and diplomacy, too often deception and imperial hubris have underscored U.S. foreign policy. We really shouldn't wonder why the Arab world hates the United States, but because we have been taught a watered-down version of history, and we've been dumbed-down into near oblivion, we don't know any better. We continue to abrogate our reasoning and formulate our consensus based upon politically biased cable news. We sadly opt to allow corporate funded intellectual elites in the media to do the thinking for us. These masterful propagandists often promote dubious policies under the guise of healthy nationalism.

In an article by Steve LaTulippe entitled, "America, Iran, and Operation Ajax: The Burden of the Past," he beautifully sums up the peril of our blissful collective ignorance in America. He said,

> The news has been abuzz recently with stories about President Bush's alleged plans for "regime change" in Iran. Just last week, rumors were reported of U.S. Air Force fighters violating Iranian air space for the purposes of testing their air defense system. As the nuclear crisis continues to simmer, the next incursions may be of a more belligerent nature.

Obviously, America's relationship with Iran has been extremely hostile over the past several decades. From the perspective of most Americans, the seminal event of U.S.-Iranian relations was the siege of the U.S. embassy in Tehran and the subsequent holding of its staff as hostages back in the 1970s.

Although that hostage taking was brutal and unjustified, many Americans lack a more global perspective of the history of American interactions with Persia. One of the most critical events in that relationship occurred over 50 years ago during the Eisenhower Administration. While Americans may know little about Operation Ajax, its memory still evokes intense anger from nearly every Iranian (LaTulippe 2005).

Indeed, many of the problems America has had over the last 50 years — the Iran/Contra Affair, the hostage taking, the Islamic revolution, and terrorism against the West — are all by-products of the Eisenhower NSC and the CIA's overthrow of Mossadeq in 1953.

But the right-wing controlled cable TV news media tells you they hate us because they are jealous of us. This chapter will hopefully shed vital new light on both — the truth behind the overthrow of a popularly elected Iranian prime minister, and on those issues that remain crucial to the evolution of relations between the United States and the so-called Axis of Evil: Iraq, Iran, and North Korea.

It is my hope that more Americans will continue to question the national security ramifications of these kinds of black operations, along with the doctrines of preemption and unilateralism in U.S. foreign policy by the extreme political right-wing.

The Great Red Scare

The antithetical rival to capitalism during the latter half of the 20th century was Communism. During that Cold War era, the word "Communist" was the most dreaded label in the English language. If someone called the average American a Communist, even in jest, it made him or her feel uneasy, to say the least.

J. Edgar Hoover used that label to try to assassinate the character of many people in this country, from Frank Sinatra to Martin Luther King to anyone else that Hoover disliked. A U.S. senator named Joseph McCarthy publicly proclaimed that there were more than two hundred "card-carrying" Communists in the United States government. Eventually, his accusations of Communist infiltration were proven false, and the Senate ultimately censured him for unbecoming conduct. Nevertheless, his zealous crusade, often referred to as "the great red scare," ushered in a near incommensurable period of contemporary repression in the 20th century American political debate.

This internal repression during the red scare period was a structural and psychological component of our foreign policy. It was vital in advancing U.S. national security interests. What do I mean? Just as McCarthy would label certain individuals as Communists whenever they didn't conform to his idea of what a good American was, the NSC would use that same label for foreign governments that were deemed a threat to Western corporate and financial interests.

From the late 1940s down to the late 1960s, the American government was consumed with concerns about the spread of Communism in Latin America, the Caribbean, Eastern Europe, China, and Vietnam. Keep in mind, John F. Kennedy said in his inaugural address, "And let every other power know that this Hemisphere intends to remain the master of its own house" (Kennedy 1961). In other words, America could not abide a Communist beachhead in the Western hemisphere. Therefore, the National Security Council could simply use the infamous label (Communist) as justification for implementing regime change by any means necessary. Sometimes it included the creation of counterfeit mobs, election rigging, and even political assassination to overthrow targeted governments.

The NSC and the CIA during the Eisenhower years used the purported threat of Communism, allegedly within Mossadeq's government, to compromise the very notion of democracy in Iran. That label would be used to justify regime change in the name of American national security. But the reality was, Mossadeq had no Communists in his government. His only crime was that he was the first nationalist to rule contemporary Persia. As such, he took control of Iran's oil away from the West. As Steven LaTulippe said in "America, Iran, and Operation Ajax: The Burden of the Past,"

> In 1951, the control of Iran's oil fields by a British company (the Anglo-Iranian Oil Company, or AIOC) became a hot political topic. The Iranian people believed, with some justification, that the existing deal between the Iranian government and

AIOC unfairly benefited the company. Muhammad Mossadeq, then a member of the Iranian parliament, took the lead in demanding a renegotiation of the pact. The masses of the Iranian people rallied to his standard and quickly made him the most revered leader in the land (LaTulippe 2005).

The 1953 Iranian Coup

After nationalizing Iran's oil industry in 1951, the democratically elected Iranian Prime Minister Mohammed Mossadeq paid the ultimate political price for stepping on the toes of American and British oil interests — he was overthrown in a violent coup orchestrated by the CIA and British intelligence in 1953. If the American people would ever question why Mossadeq was targeted for removal, they would understand one major reason that the Arab world hates and distrusts us. If this country would ask: What did Mossadeq do that would be viewed as such a threat to the national security interests of the United States and Great Britain that it would require these two great democracies to sabotage a rare example of democracy within the Middle East, we would understand the true roots of Islamic extremism.

The United States government said that Mossadeq was a Communist. Again, I ask, was this true? According to Monsurer Farhong, a student activist and a Mossadeq supporter working in Iran, Mossadeq was not a Communist. From Farhong's vantage point, he could easily determine whether or not Iran was a Communist stronghold.

In a book by Bill Moyers called The Secret Government: The Constitution in Crises, he refers to a comment made by Farhong when asked about whether or not Mossadeq supported Communists in Iran. He replied, "He did not receive an iota of assistance from the Soviet Union. In those days, in the early 50s, the idea of an independent, neutral state was unacceptable to either the United States or the Soviet Union. Mossadeq was a victim of this East/West rivalry" (Moyers 1988).

In other words, notwithstanding the grave threat that the "East/West rivalry" posed to America, the red scare was scientifically put to work in the U.S. for the purpose of generating popular support for what turned out to be imperialist policies. As long as Communism was a threat, Washington could justify doing just about anything, even the overthrow of a sovereign democratic government. On June 16, 2000, the New York Times published its PDF files of a secret CIA report by Dr. Donald N. Wilber, called "Clandestine Service History: Overthrow of Premier Mossadeq of Iran November 1952–August 1953." This operation was planned and executed by the CIA and British SIS. In it, concerning the policy of government overthrows by the United States, Dr. Wilber said,

> In 1953, Kermit Roosevelt and a few other CIA operatives organized a successful coup against Prime Minister Muhammad Mossadeq, whom the United States saw as becoming increasingly alienated from the West and more closely allied with the Soviet-dominated Tudeh Party. To prepare the way for the coup, Roosevelt

eventually secured the reluctant support of the Shah (who signed firmans [royal decrees] dismissing Mossadeq and appointing Gen. Fazollah A. Zahedi, a high-ranking officer who had been selected to spearhead the group as prime minister) and that of influential mullahs and key military leaders. Roosevelt also recruited a number of Iranian agents, including some who had formerly been in the employ of the British Secret Intelligence Service, which was involved in the planning of the coup. (Wilbur 1954).

I know all of this may seem hard to believe, but nevertheless, it's true. Understand that Dr. Donald N. Wilber was a CIA spy, who worked undercover as a Persian architectural expert. He planned the coup in Iran. Therefore, I think he should be considered an important authority on what happened. For those who still are not convinced, I would point them to chapter three of a book called Operations Against Enemy Leaders, by Stephen T. Hosmer, which describes a chilling account of the doctrines of subversion, sabotage, and total abandonment of fair play, all of which have been enacted by the National Security Council against America's enemies. In chapter three, Hosmer wrote that the U.S. government's assumptions and underlying support for coups and rebellions required that:

The United States might also act to remove or intimidate hostile leaders by attempting to facilitate their overthrow in coups or rebellion. In sanctioning military and other support to a coup or rebellion, U.S. decision makers might anticipate the following:

- U.S. assistance would be sufficient to make an otherwise problematic coup or rebellion successful.

- The successor government installed after the overthrow would adopt policies and behavior more acceptable to the United States.

- Even if the hostile regime was not overthrown, the perception of the threats posed by continued coup plotting or by a U.S.-supported rebel force would provide the United States with bargaining leverage.

- In the event that U.S. forces became engaged in combat with the forces of the enemy regime, any enemy resources diverted to guard against a threatened coup or rebellion would weaken the enemy's front-line fighting capacity (Hosmer 2001).

By now you should understand the almost limitless lengths that the United States government went to at that time to assure its hegemony, and at the same time, to assuage the unquenchable greed of a few. All Prime Minister Mossadeq simply wanted was for Iran to enjoy a fair profit from its vast oil reserves. I think it's sad that in the pursuit of power, sometimes nationalism, patriotism, and humanism take a backseat to plutocracy. Mossadeq had oil, America and Great Britain wanted it, and they took it. The aftershocks of the 1953 coup in Iran are still being felt today throughout the Islamic world and probably will continue to be felt well into the future. But this was the first of many extreme right-wing ideologically inspired CIA covert operations against foreign governments in the name of national security.

A Brief History of Oil Production in Iran

Oil production in Iran had its origins in 1901, when a wealthy Englishman, William Knox D'Arcy, combed the Iranian desert in search of oil. Seven years later in 1908, he found oil in southwest Persia. One year later, the Anglo-Persian Oil Company was formed. But by then, most of the company was owned by the Burma Oil Company.

In preparation for World War I, the Anglo-Persian Oil Company found both a premium backer and customer in Winston Churchill, then First Lord of the Admiralty, by promising England secure supplies of oil. The British government then acquired a controlling interest and became the de facto hidden power behind the oil company by injecting $2 million of investment capital into the Anglo-Persian Oil Company. In 1935, the company was renamed Anglo-Iranian Oil Company, after expansion and acquisition of new reserves in Canada, South America, Africa, Papua, and Europe in the post-World War I era.

In 1951, after World War II, the company was faced with a logistical crisis that threatened its very survival. This was the year that Mossadeq decided to nationalize what was at that time the largest, single, overseas investment of the British Empire, the assets of Anglo-Iranian Oil Company. The idea of military action against Mossadeq was contemplated by Britain, but they ultimately decided to implement a coup. This was bigger than mere money being on the line; whoever controls the resources of the Middle East controls the industrial development of the world. The only problem was getting President Harry Truman, who rejected the idea, to commit to regime change in Iran.

New York Times reporter Stephen Kinzer indicated that the August 19, 1953 coup in Iran was the first time that the U.S. government overthrew another government. Based upon the shallow nature of the intelligence and the seemingly knee-jerk decision to invade, the current Iraq war is merely the most recent example of the same thing.

These two events, initiated in the name of America's national security, have notable similarities. Not only was the motivation for the 1953 overthrow of Mohammad Mossadeq, Iran's democratically elected prime minister, mandated by the same risky geopolitical objectives as the current Iraq war, it, likewise, also inspired a worldwide militant Islamic movement using acts of terror as their tactical approach.

The Political, Strategic, and Human Compromises of the Coup

Kinzer's book, All the Shah's Men, gives us a compelling look at the 1953 coup and its political consequences. Kinzer quotes Harry Truman saying, "There is nothing new in the world except the history you do not know" (Kinzer 2003).

Kinzer clearly understands and knows what many Americans don't know or understand, that Democrat President Truman was a wise man for choosing containment over regime change. He also understands that his presidential successor, Republican Dwight D. Eisenhower, was not so wise for supporting the coup. Were there political reasons that led Ike to endorse this 180-degree policy shift?

From a political perspective, Ike wanted to counter what the hawkish cold warriors on his staff believed to be Truman's weaknesses in the face of the Soviet threat. In the case of Truman, the risks in pulling off a successful coup on behalf of the interests of the UK were high and very unpopular for Democrats facing an election. But with the elections behind him, Dwight Eisenhower, as America's new President, signed off on one of the CIA's first covert operations against a foreign government. The actions of the NSC and the CIA under Eisenhower initiated a game of geostrategic chess between East and West. The chessboard would be the volatile and oil-rich Middle East.

Republican President Eisenhower allowed the CIA to use counterfeit mobs, bribery, threats, and intimidation to create a popular uprising within Iran to overthrow Mossadeq. Hundreds of people were beaten or killed as mobs spread terror in the streets of Tehran. As a result, Mossadeq would not only be overthrown, but he would be sentenced to three years in prison, followed by house arrest for life. After the coup, the Anglo-Iranian Oil Company changed its name to one that is very familiar in contemporary America, British Petroleum (BP).

The CIA-inspired coup against Iran's first democratic government ushered in a two-decade long period of dictatorship under the Shah. The dictatorship relied heavily on U.S. aid and arms. But for every action, there is a reaction; the anti-American backlash that toppled the Shah in 1979 created widespread social instability throughout the entire region and helped spread Islamic militancy.

With virtually no other safe haven on earth after the 1979 revolution, President Jimmy Carter allowed the deposed Shah into the United States. Fearing the Shah would be sent back to take over Iran as had happened in 1953, Iranian militants took over the U.S. embassy. This was where the 1953 coup was staged. It's crystal clear that the Iranians were sending Washington a 444-daylong message, and they were using Westerners held hostage to send it. The message was: We remember what you did to us, and we will make you pay.

The 50th anniversary of the coup was front-page news in Iranian newspapers. The Christian Science Monitor reports one paper in Iran publishing excerpts from CIA documents on the coup that had been released only three years earlier. At that time, the U.S. involvement in the fall of Mossadeq was still not publicly acknowledged.

Nevertheless, in a New York Times article in March 2000, Secretary of State Madeleine Albright openly admitted, "The coup was clearly a setback for Iran's political development. And it is easy to see now why many Iranians continue to resent this intervention by America in their internal affairs" (Albright 2000).

I say, not only do Iranians resent America's interventionism and deceptive diplomacy, the entire Islamic world resents our Middle East policies. In fact, Prof. Ervand Abrahamian tells us in Khomeinism: Essays on the Islamic Republic, "Muslims, Khomeini insisted, have the sacred duty to oppose all monarchies. They must not collaborate with them, have recourse to their institutions, pay for their bureaucracies, or practice dissimulation to protect themselves. On the contrary, they have the duty to rise up (qiyam) against them. Most kings, he added, have been criminals, oppressors, and mass murderers" (Abrahamian 1993).

Although America is not ruled by a monarchy, because of actions like Operation Ajax, we are viewed as the kinds of criminals, oppressors, and mass murderers that Khomeini wanted to destroy. In his book All the Shah's Men, Kinzer gives America a sober warning: "It is not far-fetched to draw a line from Operation Ajax (the name of the coup) through the Shah's repressive regime and the Islamic Revolution to the fireballs that engulfed the World Trade Center in New York" (Kinzer 2003).

Chapter Five

★ ★ ★ ★ ★

Operation Success

The Lessons of 1954

On May 23, 1997, the CIA finally released previously classified documents on its involvement in the infamous 1954 coup in Guatemala. For years, the CIA had avoided answering Freedom of Information Act requests with the standard mantra, "We can neither confirm nor deny that such records exist." It took 43 years for the CIA to declassify approximately less than 1.5 percent of the estimated 100,000 pages in its secret archives on its covert program to destabilize and topple the Guatemalan government in 1954. This is hardly the kind of transparency necessary to counter the rise of a secret government in America.

The CIA director at the time was Robert Gates. Mr. Gates promised that the CIA would open its secret post-Cold War activities to public scrutiny. But he was obviously planning to only crack open the door just a tiny little bit, because only a couple of days later, a member of the CIA's own historical review panel was quoted in the New York Times as calling the CIA's promised transparency "a brilliant public relations snow job" (Weiner 1997).

The question should be, How can we learn anything from the past when we're not told what happened? Why do they continue to try to snow the American people? The lessons are much the same as what we should have learned from the 1953 coup in Iran, but, unfortunately, we still haven't taken any of these lessons to heart.

Quite frankly, it seems to me that no matter how many times extreme right-wing elements within our government trashes the Constitution, substantive activism from the American people and their elected representatives is still insufficient to check the unbridled avarice of the extreme Right.

Not long ago, you could attribute ignorance and indifference to this problem. Today, thanks to aggressive momentum toward a more authoritarian government in post-911 America, you must include the fear and smear tactics of political extremists toward suppression of dissent. Too many good people who know better are afraid to speak out, both inside and outside the government. Those who do speak out are too often trivialized, vilified, or ignored. We should remember the admonishment of President Kennedy who said,

The men who create power make an indispensable contribution to the nation's greatness. But the men who question power make a contribution just as indispensable, especially when that questioning is disinterested, for they determine whether we use power or power uses us (Kennedy 1963).

People allowed themselves to be used and abused by power itself during the German empire's First Reich from 1871 to 1919; also during the Second Reich from 1919 to 1933 in the Weimar Republic. Again, power totally arrested egalitarianism during the Third Reich from 1933 to 1945. We must learn the lessons of Germany from 1871–1945, and we must also learn the lessons from Guatemala in 1954. Then we must practically apply this knowledge today and not allow the various skirmish lines in the so-called war of terror to cause our liberty to be sacrificed. We must never allow the United States of America to become the Fourth Reich. Always question power.

The Arbenz Government

Recently, television evangelist and former presidential candidate Pat Robertson got into big trouble with evangelicals all across America for suggesting that the United States should assassinate President Hugo Chavez of Venezuela. The mere suggestion of official sanctioning of a political assassination by the U.S. government made Robertson politically radioactive. Well, if you like what Robertson suggested, you're going to love what the CIA and the NSC were doing in Guatemala in the early 1950s.

On March 15, 1951, Jaboco Arbenz became president of Guatemala. The flame of democracy burned bright in Guatemala for Arbenz. With the support of 65 percent of the voters giving him their approval, Arbenz and his nationalistic policies held great excitement. He campaigned on a promise to continue a process of socioeconomic and nationalistic reforms. But these reforms would set Arbenz at odds with powerful financial and industrial interests in the United States, and the CIA would be called upon to do something to stop it. In its 1997 declassified memoranda, the CIA referred to the policy platform of Arbenz as "an intensely nationalistic program of progress colored by the touchy, anti-foreign inferiority complex of the Banana Republic" (Doyle and Kornbluh 1997).

Arbenz began his work of reforms immediately. His first action was to begin building a new seaport. Shipping was very lucrative then as it is today, and having a port under Guatemalan control would allow the people of Guatemala to compete with United Fruit's privatized facility, the Puerto Barrios. That was strike one.

Next, he tried to bust the transportation monopoly of the International Railways of Central America (IRCA) with his own ambitious transportation project. Like shipping by sea, shipping by land is very lucrative and having a new highway to the Atlantic built and controlled by the Guatemalan government was unwanted competition for the IRCA. That's strike two.

Arbenz also wanted to rid Guatemala of energy dependence on the United States. So he decided to build a nationally controlled hydroelectric plant to offer a cheaper energy alternative from the American-controlled electricity monopoly. Energy is an extremely lucrative sector in any market, and nationalizing that commodity cost private interests in the U.S. a lot of money. That was strike three.

But we are the USA, and we are the good guys, so you know we gave him a few more strikes before we finally had enough and crushed him.

By then, the policies of the new Guatemalan president had become extremely problematic for American financial interests, but he still wasn't done slapping the lion in the face. In addition to the kind of infrastructural sovereignty changes Arbenz was making, he also proposed a new system of progressive income tax designed to reduce his dependence on foreign loans. Remember, a bank makes money by collecting interest from debt. If Guatemala was allowed to develop a self-sustaining socioeconomic infrastructure, they might eventually throw off the shackles of debt slavery to foreign banks. Strike four.

The final straw that broke the camel's back came when Arbenz began to try to correct Guatemala's unequal land distribution. He said that Guatemala needed "an agrarian reform which puts an end to the latifundios and the semi-feudal practices giving the land to thousands of peasants, raising their purchasing power and creating a great internal market favorable to the development of domestic industry" (Spartacus Educational).

The land reform was approved in 1952, empowering the Guatemalan government to distribute this expropriated land only to landless peasants in 42.5-acre plots each. The plots could not be sold, and the new owners would pay a rental fee to the government in the amount of 5 percent of the value of the food they produced.

The problem with this plan was that this new Agrarian Reform initiative required the nationalization of 85 percent of privatized land assets of the United Fruit Company (UFC). The government then gave 1.5 million acres of land to approximately 100,000 peasant families in Guatemala. The government very cleverly financed this reform with a little more than $8 million in bonds, compromising American banks and the UFC.

Now the Americans were really starting to get pissed off. The UFC owned 550,000 acres on the Atlantic coast, and almost half of it (209,842 acres) was taken away under this Agrarian Reform initiative in March of 1953. The Guatemalan government offered the UFC $525,000 ($2.99 per acre) to compensate them for their loss, but the UFC insisted upon $16 million for the land ($75 per acre).

I think the Guatemalan offer to American business interests was a much better deal than the United States government offered to Native-Americans in the 19th century. Arbenz could have simply said get the hell out of my country. Still, this was strike five, and it was time to do something about it.

The 1954 Guatemala Coup

The United Fruit Company's largest shareholder was a man named Samuel Zemurray. Mr. Zemurray was livid. He knew that the U.S. government had to get involved if Arbenz was going to be stopped. But before the American government could get involved, he had to make the American people believe that Arbenz was a threat to, you guessed it, national security. Zemurray sponsored an anti-Arbenz campaign in the American media, claiming that Guatemala was a part of "Soviet expansion in the Americas" (Spartacus Educational). This is when the CIA became involved.

The CIA's top dog for this case was Frank Wisner, head of the Office of Policy Coordination. Richard Bissell, head of the Directorate for Plans, who had been in charge of covert anti-Communist operations all over the world, was also involved. This "Executive Action" (a plan to remove unfriendly foreign leaders from power) under the right-wing government of President Dwight D. Eisenhower became known as "Operation Success." Wisner harnessed the best anti-Communists and Cold War propagandists at the CIA to run Operation Success (OS). In charge of OS was Tracy Barnes, who convinced David Atlee Phillips to take charge of the propaganda campaign.

In Phillips's autobiography The Night Watch, the author obviously felt that what the CIA was doing in Guatemala wasn't right. He told Barnes, "But Arbenz became President in a free election. What right do we have to help someone topple his government and throw him out of office?" (Phillips 1977). But when Barnes told him that Arbenz was a Communist sympathizer, he knew we had to fall in line because if the Soviets established a "beachhead in Central America" (Phillips 1977), it would pose a threat to America's national security.

The Psychological Operations Begin

The CIA propaganda campaign went into full swing. They published 100,000 copies of a pamphlet entitled Chronology of Communism in Guatemala. In movie theatres all across America, three films on Guatemala were showing for free. David Atlee Phillips, along with E. Howard Hunt, also launched a talk radio campaign against Arbenz. The CIA operated a radio station called The Voice of Liberation, where Phillips and Hunt made sure Arbenz got pounded, just like the talk-show hosts of today's extreme Right pound Democrats in America. Posters and cartoons were produced to further generate their anti-Arbenz hysteria. The CIA even used faked photographs showing mutilated bodies, which were said to be opponents of Arbenz.

The CIA also used a very zealous "Executive Action" agent named William "RIP" Robertson in its campaign against Arbenz. Robertson was an assassinations asset of the CIA, who worked on the Arbenz case when assassinating the leader was still on the table. There is also photographic evidence of "RIP" Robertson in Dealey Plaza on November 22, 1963, during the Kennedy assassination.

The CIA's Covert Proxy Army

The CIA's efforts at overthrowing Arbenz would not stop with psychological operations. As I mentioned, at one point, assassination was on the table. But with the logistical help of the brutal Nicaraguan dictator, Anastasio Somoza, the CIA then began spending $20 million on a proxy army, trained in Nicaragua and led by Colonel Carlos Castillo.

Now the CIA's squeeze was really on in Guatemala. The situation there was so intense that Guatemala had to ask the United Nations to help. The foreign minister in Guatemala, Guillermo Toriello, told UN officials that the insistence on the U.S. government's characterization "as Communism for every manifestation of nationalism or economic independence, any desire for social progress, any intellectual curiosity, and any interest in progressive liberal reforms" (Spartacus Educational) was unwarranted and unjust.

With the eyes of the world on the U.S. for a response, or an explanation, the U.S. ambassador to Guatemala confirmed that the U.S. viewed Guatemala as a Communist nation, saying, "We cannot permit a Soviet Republic to be established between Texas and the Panama Canal" (Spartacus Educational).

Eisenhower said that Arbenz was a "Communist dictator" who had "established an outpost on this continent to the detriment of all the American nations" (Spartacus Educational).

Secretary of State John Foster Dulles responded by saying that Arbenz sponsors a "Communist type of terrorism" (Spartacus Educational).

Thanks to the work of another Republican, Henry Cabot Lodge, the UN Security Council resolution to investigate Toriello's claims was narrowly defeated due to intense pressure on members from the United States. Now Arbenz was naked. The appalling silence of the world as democracy was threatened in this case only affirms how effectual and successful the extreme Right has been in their methods of modifying and garnering the consent of those who know better.

Now America's proxy army, under the bloodthirsty leadership of Carlos Castillo, could be unleashed upon the peasants of Guatemala. The CIA started bribing Arbenz's officers into surrendering their troops. Castillo's forces then crossed the Honduran–Guatemalan border, as the CIA's "Voice of Liberation" broadcasts worked to tactically support them with artful propaganda.

Even though Castillo's army was smaller than the Guatemalan army, the propaganda radio broadcasts ate away at Arbenz's support by telling them that two large groups of invaders were moving towards Guatemala City, and the fall of Guatemala was imminent. When Arbenz's army had finally been bribed and scared into surrender, and when the CIA successfully blocked the formation of civilian militias, allowing hundreds of their fellow citizens to be killed in the coup, Arbenz announced his resignation over the radio.

The Aftermath of the Coup

The truth of the matter is that Guatemala was not a Communist government. Arbenz did allow all political parties to participate, but there were only 4 out of 51 seats in the Guatemalan government that were held by Communists. After Arbenz left power, the diplomatic isolationism and confrontational posture from the U.S. toward Guatemala under Arbenz instantly changed with the recognition of the Castillo government by Eisenhower. The net result was that

Castillo gave back all the land that Arbenz took from the United Fruit Company, along with reversing the rest of Arbenz's reforms.

Over the next few weeks, beginning on July 19, 1954, thousands of Arbenz's supporters were rounded up and tossed into prison as suspected Communists. Many of them were tortured, and some were even killed. The new government destroyed all voting rights, trade unions, a free independent press, and peasant organizations. Any dissent brought on swift incarceration, torture, or death. From that time on, Arbenz moved around from country to country, all over Europe and Latin America, staying only short periods of time, until he was found dead in his bathtub. He allegedly drowned.

The United States had not only subverted democracy in Guatemala, but it had caused the deaths of thousands of innocent people. All this was done in the name of national security. As Marine Colonel Phillip Roettinger, who was recruited to join the CIA's team on Operation Success, said in The Secret Government: The Constitution in Crises, by Bill Moyers, "What we did has caused a succession of repressive military dictatorships in that country and has been responsible for the death of over 100,000 of their citizens" (Moyers 1989).

All of this happened because the greed of a few people and the massive abuse of government power under the national security mandate made it possible. The truth is, Arbenz was never a threat to our national security. The real threat to our national security was, and usually always is, greed. It seems that nothing can satisfy the greed of some members of the elite ruling class in America. When anyone or anything gets in the way of their plutocratic agenda, they have at their disposal an infrastructure of right-wing drones and zealots in politics, the media, banking, and corporate industrial America to vanquish their adversaries with the cunning and brutality of an African lion.

Chapter Six

★ ★ ★ ★ ★

Project FUBELT

The Lessons of 1973

It's amazing how the American people allowed a single word, "Communism," to make us surrender so much. What did we surrender, you say? We won the Cold War, so what did we surrender? We surrendered our wealth, our image, and our peace of mind. But perhaps the most egregious loss was America's war powers, which are delegated to Congress by the Constitution.

Whenever Communism was said to be a threat, shadowy forces operating from the back door of one administration after another, usually the political Right, have unconstitutionally assumed absolute authority through the use of executive privilege. Under the national security state, secret operatives from various administrations, Left and Right, have taken the liberty to secretly carry out their own illegal, covert operations. Usually when they have done this, their actions have resulted in assassinations, drug running, and coups, to name but a few. In general, destabilizing and destroying peace on earth has too often been the sullen hallmark of their activities.

The average person in America hasn't a clue as to what's going on within the hazy world of the national security state. Questions such as, why are these actions taken, how are these kinds of operations financed, or how much is being spent, are not publicly asked, and many of those who do think about them are afraid to ask.

But by 1975, the United States Senate began to ask some of those questions. They began to publicly look into the CIA's covert activities. The country now got a glimpse inside the dark, shadowy activities of the national security state.

Democrat Senator Frank Church, a strong critic of the Vietnam War, was chairman of the Select Committee to Study Government Operations. Those hearings exposed a long line of deadly and illegal actions by the American intelligence community, both in and outside of the United States. To accomplish the foreign policy objectives of the national security state when diplomacy wouldn't work and direct U.S. military operations were not politically viable, the CIA's covert operations could be mobilized without congressional consent.

Church gave us a shocking glimpse into Nixon's secret 1973 campaign to overthrow the government in Chile. In

The Secret Government: The Constitution in Crises by Bill Moyers, Church was quoted in 1976 as saying,

> Like Caesar peering into the colonies from distant Rome, Nixon said the choice of government by the Chileans was unacceptable to the President of the United States. The attitude in the White House seemed to be, "If in the wake of Vietnam I can no longer send in the Marines, then I will send in the CIA" (Moyers 1988).

That is exactly what happened in Chile from 1970 to 1973. The President of the United States in 1973, Richard M. Nixon, saw the government in Chile and their president, Salvador Allende, as an "unacceptable" problem. So it was time to call in the CIA and give Chile their own 911. On September 11, 1973, a CIA-sponsored military coup toppled Allende's government from power. Salvador Allende was assassinated during the fighting in the presidential palace in Santiago. General Augusto Pinochet replaced the fallen Allende as president.

The men who wrote the U.S. Constitution were wise and smart enough not to intend to bestow the kind of unilateral executive power to the office of the President that we have witnessed since the passage of the National Security Act of 1947. So what is the biggest lesson of the 1973 Chilean coup? What are the voices from the graves and the blood-soaked Chilean soil trying to tell us? They scream for us to stop allowing even the appearance of contempt for the rule of law by our government, which has become so characteristic of the national security state.

Democracy in Chile

Chile gained its independence from Spain in 1818 the same way America gained its independence from England, through war and bloodshed. The Chilean War of Independence was part of San Martín's War in South America, which lasted for eight bloody years from 1810 to 1818.

General José de San Martín and General Bernardo O'Higgins led their combined Argentinean and Chilean forces across the Andes in January 1817. On February 12, 1817, these two brave generals and their army of nearly 5,000 soldiers defeated the mighty Spanish and colonial army at the Battle of Chacabuco. Three days later, they took the city of Santiago. A succession of skirmishes with the Spanish would ensue over the following year. Ultimately, after suffering heavy losses and being forced to retreat to Peru, the Spanish army fell, allowing Chile to proclaim its independence on February 12, 1818.

From that day forward, democracy began to evolve in Chile, just as it evolved in the United States. By 1861, democracy had been fully achieved in Chile, making it one of the most powerful states in Latin America. Throughout the history of democracy in Chile, internal clashes between liberal civilian and conservative military forces threatened its survival. Nevertheless, democracy endured.

A very popular liberal politician named Arturo Alessandri introduced social reforms in the 1920s and 1930s. In general, liberal social reforms will always find opposition by the rich and those who hold power within the state.

Just like the United States, conservatives in Chile, particularly the military, vehemently opposed any reforms designed to create a more activist government on behalf of the working-class people. The rich have always fought against a more egalitarian allocation of resources between the rich and the poor.

But alas, even in the face of opposition from its own military and covert influence and manipulation from the CIA in their elections going back to 1958, Chile remained a democratic country. The Right, Left, and all aspects between enjoyed a complex and shaky truce, allowing political power to be shared from the end of World War II thru the end of the 1960s.

In 1970, a historic election in Chile allowed the first Marxist in world history to ascend to power in an open and free democratic election when Salvador Allende, the leader of the Chilean Socialist Party, was elected president. It should be pointed out that although the Chilean Socialist Party, which Allende helped establish in 1933, was a Marxist organization, they did not approve of the Soviet Union's Communist Party.

The fact that Chile did elect a Marxist, combined with the fact that he was elected by such a small margin, only 36.2 percent, reflected the difficulty in achieving cross-ideological political coalescence. In other words, Chile, like America today, was ideologically and politically polarized.

Nixon's Chilean Covert Operations, 1970

As I've already mentioned, the CIA had been conducting covert operations in Chile since the late 1950s. According to a staff report of the Select Committee to Study Governmental Operations with Respect to Intelligence Activities, which was chaired by Senator Frank Church, called "Covert Action in Chile 1963–1973," the undermining of democracy in the name of U.S. national security is officially confirmed. An excerpt from the report reads as follows:

> Early in 1969, President Nixon announced a new policy toward Latin America, labeled by him "Action for Progress." It was to replace the "Alliance for Progress," which the President characterized as paternalistic and unrealistic. Instead, the United States was to seek "mature partnership" with Latin American countries, emphasizing trade and not aid. The reformist trappings of the Alliance were to be dropped; the United States announced itself prepared to deal with foreign governments pragmatically.
>
> The United States program of covert action in the 1970 Chilean elections reflected this less activist stance. Nevertheless, that covert involvement was substantial. In March 1970, the 40 Committee decided that the United States should not support any single candidate in the election but should instead wage "spoiling" operations against the Popular Unity coalition which supported the Marxist candidate, Salvador Allende. In all, the CIA spent from $800,000 to $1,000,000 on covert action to affect the outcome

of the 1970 presidential election. Of this amount, about half was for major efforts approved by the 40 Committee. By CIA estimates, the Cubans provided about $350,000 to Allende's campaign, with the Soviets adding an additional, undetermined amount.

The "spoiling" operations had two objectives: (1) undermining communist efforts to bring about a coalition of leftist forces which could gain control of the presidency in 1970; and (2) strengthening non-Marxist political leaders and forces in Chile to order to develop an effective alternative to the Popular Unity coalition in preparation for the 1970 presidential election.

In working toward these objectives, the CIA made use of half-a-dozen covert action projects. Those projects were focused into an intensive propaganda campaign which made use of virtually all media within Chile and which placed and replayed items in the international press as well. Propaganda placements were achieved through subsidizing right-wing women's and "civic action" groups. A "scare campaign" equated an Allende victory with violence and Stalinist repression.

In addition to the massive propaganda campaign, the CIA's effort prior to the election included political action aimed at splintering the non-Marxist Radical Party and reducing the number of votes which it could deliver to the Popular Unity coalition's candidate. Also, "black propaganda" — material purporting to be the product of another group — was used in 1970 to sow dissent between Communists and Socialists, and between the national labor confederation and the Chilean Community Party.

The CIA's propaganda operation for the 1970 elections made use of mechanisms that had been developed earlier. One mechanism had been used extensively by the CIA during the March 1969 congressional elections. During the 1970 campaign, it produced hundreds of thousands of high-quality printed pieces, ranging from posters and leaflets to picture books, and carried out an extensive propaganda program through many radio and press outlets. Other propaganda mechanisms that were in place prior to the 1970 campaign included an editorial support group that provided political features, editorials, and news articles for radio and press placement; a service for placing anti-communist press and radio items; and three different news services.

There was a wide variety of propaganda products: a newsletter mailed to approximately two thousand journalists, academicians, politicians, and other opinion makers; a booklet showing what life would be like if Allende won the presidential election; translation and distribution of chronicles of opposition to the Soviet regime; poster distribution and sign-painting teams. The sign-painting teams had instructions to paint the slogan "su paredon" (your wall) on 2,000 walls, evoking an image of communist firing squads. The "scare campaign" (campaña de terror) exploited the violence of the invasion of Czechoslovakia with large photographs of Prague and of tanks in downtown Santiago. Other posters portrayed Cuban political prisoners before the firing squad and warned that an Allende victory would mean the end of religion and family life in Chile.

Still another project funded individual press assets. One, who produced regular radio commentary shows on a nationwide hookup, continued to wage propaganda for the CIA during the Allende presidency. Other assets, all employees of El Mercurio, enabled the station to generate more than one editorial per day based on CIA guidance. Access to El Mercurio had a multiplier effect since its editorials were read throughout the country on various national radio networks. Moreover, El Mercurio was one of the most influential Latin American newspapers, particularly in business circles abroad. A project which placed anti-Communist press and radio items was reported in 1970 to reach an audience of well over five million listeners.

The CIA funded only one political group during the 1970 campaign in an effort to reduce the number of Radical Party votes for Allende (Staff report of the Select Committee to Study Governmental Operations with Respect to Intelligence Activities 1975).

This was a classic case of influencing the outcome of an election on foreign soil by the U.S. Central Intelligence

Agency. The impact of these activities is nearly impossible to calculate because much of the dollars spent on financing the CIA covert operations could be channeled through the Chilean black market, where the unofficial exchange rate into Chilean Escudos often reached five times the official rate. Just like in America where a bad candidate can easily win an election when he or she has vastly more amounts of money than the opponent, so it was in Chile.

The world hasn't forgotten about the CIA's activity in Chile, and it is one of the main reasons why other countries are so skeptical about American-inspired involvement in their political affairs. It's not the freedom to choose at which other countries bristle; it's manipulation of the choices by Americans that they dread. Our neighbors in the developing world have enough problems of their own to contend with. But as Allende found out, the CIA can add additional straws and eventually break the camel's back.

Additional Problems for Allende

There must be something special about government of, by, and for the people, because in spite of all that the Nixon White House did to try to subvert the election and stop Allende from being elected, he won. But the psychological damage done to Chile was a compromise against its stability that would last long after the election.

The other problems Allende had to face, on top of all of the CIA's so-called spoiling operations against his Popular Unity coalition during the election, concerned Chile's formidable economic maladies: Monetary reform was considered as Chile's currency faced hyperinflation, over 20 percent of the male adult population was unemployed, and approximately half of the children under 15 suffered from malnutrition.

Allende's policies worked well during his first year in office, but efforts by the West to destabilize his country took a serious toll during his final two years. According to the Popular Unity Coalition, foreign and domestic capitalists were exploiting Chile. They had become likened unto vampires, sucking the wealth right out of the country, leaving the poor economically emaciated. Allende implemented immediate nationalistic economic reforms. He nationalized the copper mines, which were owned by two United States companies, Kennecott and Anaconda. He also took over various foreign-held firms, industries, banks, and lands. Allende also decided to return the nationalized lands to the people of Chile and raise wages by 40 percent. Then he reopened diplomatic relations with Cuba, China, and the German Democratic Republic.

Allende's nationalism was diametrically opposed to the privatization sought by capitalists in and out of Chile. Too much nationalism anywhere in the Western hemisphere is a threat to privatization everywhere in the Western hemisphere. Those powerful financial interests in the North didn't want to allow their other weaker subjects in the South to imitate that kind of liberation from their domination. As William Blum put it in *Killing Hope: U.S. Military and CIA interventions since World War II*,

What was there about Salvador Allende that warranted all this feverish activity? What threat did he represent, this man against whom the great technical and economic resources of the world's most powerful nation were brought to bear? Allende was a man whose political program, as described by the Senate committee report, was to "redistribute income" [two percent of the population received 46 percent of the income] and reshape the Chilean economy, beginning with the nationalization of major industries, especially the copper companies. He also expanded agrarian reform and expanded relations with socialist and communist countries (Blum 1995).

Nationalism was a dangerous strategic move for Allende, but he made the worst possible strategic mistake in June 1973, when he appointed Augusto Pinochet commander-in-chief of the Chilean army. What Allende didn't know was that Pinochet was a contract agent with the CIA, preparing Chile's 911. With the CIA's help, Pinochet carried out a military coup against Allende's government on 9/11/1973. Allende was assassinated in his palace while fighting for his country's sovereignty.

Pinochet immediately appointed himself president, shut down the Allende government, and reversed all of Allende's reforms. Thousands of Allende sympathizers were systematically tortured, forced into exile, and murdered shortly thereafter under Pinochet's brutal, right-wing dictatorship. The Nixon White House and the CIA, operating under the auspices of the national security mandate in the United States, had finally overthrown democracy in Chile.

The CIA then poured into Chile, privatizing all the assets that Allende had nationalized. Great Britain's right-wing Thatcher government accelerated the militarization of Pinochet and scuttled any human rights reviews by the UN.

Project FUBELT was a success. It was the codename for the secret CIA operations that were intended to undermine Salvador Allende's government and promote a military coup in Chile. They successfully extinguished another fledgling democracy. Chalk up another one for the extreme Right in Washington.

Chapter Seven

★ ★ ★ ★ ★

Iran/Contra

The Lessons of 1986

Probably the most famous man in the world in the summer of 1987 was Lt. Colonel Oliver North. He made the cover of Time magazine on July 20, 1987, testifying on the Iran/Contra Affair. The caption on the cover read, "I Was Authorized to Do Everything that I Did." In that statement, at least, I believe he was telling the truth. Based upon the history of U.S. covert operations in Latin America and other parts of the world, I believe he was carrying out the plans of the President of the United States and the National Security Council in the 1980s.

The Iran/Contra Affair was one of the biggest political scandals in the history of the United States. President Ronald

Reagan used America's national security apparatus to justify a highly illegal CIA black operation. Under his administration, illegal arms sales to Iran, and even the illicit sale of drugs in the United States, were carried out by Colonel North and others conducting these covert operations through what North described as an "off the shelf, stand alone, self-sustaining entity" (Moyers 1988) called the "Enterprise."

The Enterprise had no problem with ignoring any and all restrictions passed by Congress, or having wanton disregard for the will of the people, or for trashing the Constitution of the United States. Keep in mind, these illegal arms sales to Iran came on the heels of the Khomeni Revolution.

I find it unconscionable that at a time when Iran was characterized as an enemy.of the United States, rogue elements of our government carried out such illegal activities, even though Americans were being held hostage by members of the Hezbollah in Lebanon at the time. You should remember that the Hezbollah is a Shiite Islamic terrorist organization dedicated to the ideology of the late Ayatollah Khomeni.

Although cutting this deal probably secured their release, as far as I'm concerned, it was still wrong. It was wrong because the official policy of the United States at the time, and still today, is not to cut deals with terrorists.

Today, the militant Islamic oganization, Hamas, has won a majority of seats in the Palestinian Legislative Council. The election results came in on January 26, 2006, at 12 noon EST. The Bush administration immediately announced that it would not do business with Hamas because the United States does not recognize terrorists.

If not doing business with terrorists has always been the official policy of the United States, then it was wrong during the 1980s, just as, according to the current administration, it is wrong to do business with terrorists today. But the fact remains that the United States was involved in a lot of business with terrorists in the 1980s, both in the Middle East and in Latin America. America's dealings with terrorists added greatly to the instability of the region when right-wing elements within the U.S. government began supplying Iraq with weapons of mass destruction at the same time that they were selling arms to Iran. Iraq and Iran were at war with each other, and the United States government was shamefully supplying both sides.

The Reagan administration then diverted proceeds from those illegal arms sales in the Middle East to the Contras in Latin America. The Contras were anti-Communist guerrilla insurgents, fighting against the socialist Sandinista government of Nicaragua. Both the weapons sales and the funneling of the proceeds to the Contras were against the law.

The Reagan White House violated the will of Congress, the United States Constitution, and the will of the American people. Of course, their excuse was national security. Today, Colonel North is an analyst for the FOX News network. Some on the Right have even suggested that Colonel North seek the presidency himself.

The Target Is Nicaragua

Nicaragua might not be the biggest covert action since 1947 per se, but it was big enough to cause the kinds of grotesque violations of the law that I have previously mentioned. As such, Nicaragua became the most controversial foreign policy issue in the 1980s.

Beginning in 1979, the chronic groaning for autonomy in Nicaragua finally began to materialize. In that year, the Sandinista National Liberation Front in that country successfully overthrew the 40-year dictatorship of the Somoza family and seized control of the country. This would be the main foreign policy focus for any incoming U.S. President in 1980 because for 40 years, the U.S. policy toward the Somoza regime was a policy of engagement. It didn't matter if the election that unseated the Somozas was certified as free and fair by international observers. The U.S. considered it a confrontation to American interests in the region.

After forming in 1961, the Sandinistas became very cozy with the Castro regime in Cuba. Absent of recognition by Washington, they looked to Castro for advice and support. Their pro-Communist posture continued after their new government was installed. They even began to align themselves with the Soviet Union for political, military, and economic assistance. Their strategic ties with the Soviet bloc, naturally, unsettled Washington. Having another Communist outpost could destabilize the strategic order of the hemisphere.

The last, intolerable straw breaking the proverbial camel's back, for Washington, came in 1981. In that year, the hawkish new Reagan administration learned that Castro was influencing the Sandinistas to supply arms to the Salvadoran insurgency. In spite of Nicaragua's denials of arms peddling and Communist sympathizing, the Reagan administration terminated what little aid was being given to Nicaragua. Now Nicaragua had to rely even more on Soviet bloc aid, and at the same time, suffer tremendous anxiety and fear of U.S. aggression.

But the U.S. wasn't the only nation in this half of the globe to view the Sandinistas as a threat to its national security. The Honduran government also saw the left-leaning Sandinistas as a threat and began to take action. Under the leadership of Colonel Gustavo Alvarez Martínez, chief of the Honduran armed forces, exiled members of Somoza's national guard began gathering their forces in the neighboring Honduras and Costa Rica. Martínez believed that Somoza's ex-guardsmen would be very useful assets in preventing the spread of a pro-Communist revolution into Honduras. Alvarez wanted Washington to back his plan to turn the guard into a counterrevolutionary force. All the United States would have to do is provide financial support, and Honduras would provide the base of operations.

In November 1981, Reagan allowed the CIA to begin backing the new paramilitary force, which became known as the Contras. The only problem in maintaining a green light for these operations was the Boland Amendment.

The Boland Amendment

The Contras and their counterrevolutionary cause were near and dear to President Reagan's heart. In fact, he once said he, himself, was one of them, "So I guess they are counterrevolutionary, and God bless them for being that way, and I guess that makes them Contras, and so it makes me a Contra too," (Moyers 1988) the President said.

In carrying out Reagan's desire to support the Contras, the CIA conducted a series of acts of sabotage. This was done without the Congressional Intelligence Committee giving its consent, or even being made aware of it beforehand.

The Republican-controlled Senate became enraged, leading to the passage of the Boland Amendment, which prohibited the federal government from providing military support "for the purpose of overthrowing the government of Nicaragua" (U.S. House of Representatives Appropriations Bill 1982) and subsequent, cutting off appropriated funding for the Contras.

This act deeply angered President Reagan. On one occasion, he vowed to support the Contras no matter what, saying, "As long as there is breath in this body, I will speak and work, strive and struggle, for the cause of the Nicaraguan freedom fighters" (Moyers 1988). During the visit of Pope John Paul II in Miami, Reagan, again, expressed before the so-called Vicar of Christ that "I have just made a promise to his holiness that we will not give up our struggle to support the Nicaraguan freedom fighters" (Reagan 1987). Keep in mind, Central America has long been a bastion for Roman

Catholicism. If the region went to the Communist athiests, the ensuing repression would not bode well for the church.

The Reagan camp gambled that since the Democrats in Congress lacked the votes necessary to make the Boland Amendment anything other than a compromise and not a comprehensive ban, they could maneuver through the ambiguous, but dangerous, legal waters and successfully carry out their objective. The loophole that the White House tried to navigate through was a limitation of the Boland Amendment. The amendment only banned the CIA's appropriated funds. The White House used unappropriated money spent by the National Security Council to do an end-run around Congress. Those unappropriated funds, in part, were derived from proceeds from the sale of illegal drugs on the streets of the United States.

The Drug Trade and the Enterprise

As I've said, these unappropriated funds were derived by any means necessary, including proceeds from illegal arms deals with Iran and the illegal sale of cocaine in the United States. And again, this illicit activity was carried out by the CIA. When questioned about the arms deals from America to Iran conducted by the so-called Enterprise during the Iran/Contra hearings in Congress, Colonel North exclaimed, "And I still, to this day, Council, don't see anything wrong with taking the Ayatollah's money and sending it to support the Nicaraguan Freedom Fighters" (Moyers 1988).

Trying to further expose the drug running conducted by the Enterprise that took place in the U.S. at that time, on

October 7, 1994, senior White House correspondent Sarah McClendon questioned President Bill Clinton about it. When the drug running activities were being conducted by the Enterprise during the Reagan years, Clinton was still governor of Arkansas. The reason she asked Clinton about these activities was because the Enterprise chose to use a small airfield in Mena, Arkansas, as its staging ground. She really put the President on the spot when she asked him,

> Sir, the Republicans are trying to blame you for the existence of a small airbase at Mena, Arkansas. This base was set up by George Bush and Oliver North and the CIA to help the Iran/Contras. And they brought in planeload after planeload of cocaine there for sale in the United States, and then they took the money and they bought weapons and took them back to the Contras. All of this was illegal under the Boland Act. But tell me, did they tell you that this had to be in existence because of National Security?

Appearing calm but definitely bothered that this elderly reporter would ask a question so sensitive to national security, the President answered,

> Well, let me answer the question. No, they didn't tell me anything about it. They didn't say anything to me about it. The airport in question and all the events in question were the subject of state and federal inquiries and it was found primarily a matter for federal jurisdiction. The state really had next to nothing to do with it. The local prosecutor did conduct an investigation based on what was in

the jurisdiction of state law. The rest of it was under jurisdiction of the United States attorneys appointed successively by previous administrations. We had nothing, zero, to do with it, and everybody who's ever looked into it knows that (Reed and Cummings 1995).

According to Terry Reed and John Cummings in their best-selling book, Compromised: Clinton, Bush and the CIA, Polk County Arkansas Special Prosecutor Charles Black went to then Governor Bill Clinton for funding for a grand jury investigation, saying that a thorough investigation and challenging the CIA would bankrupt rural Polk County. But it appears Governor Clinton wouldn't or couldn't help.

Keep in mind, obstructing these kinds of operations can be extremely dangerous, politically and otherwise. I know that I would hate to be governor of a state in America where the CIA had chosen to conduct this kind of black operation. I personally believe that at the time, Governor Bill Clinton did not have a choice but to allow his state to be compromised by President Reagan and the CIA. Ask yourself, would you have tried to stand in their way when the nightly news focused on the murders of individuals surrounding this covert operation?

But back to Polk County Arkansas Special Prosecutor Charles Black's request for funding, Mr. Black said, "It became apparent that nothing was going to be done about it on the federal level [when I began to more actively pursue it]. His response to me was that he would get a man on it and would get word back to me. I never heard back" (Reed and Cummings 1995).

So Clinton's statement, "The local prosecutor did conduct an investigation based upon what was within the jurisdiction of state law," may have had some truth to it, but if there was an investigation by the local prosecutor, it lacked the funding to make it successful.

Under pressure from local investigators, Clinton promised to give Special Prosecutor Charles Black $25,000 to fund the investigation. According to Reed and Cummings, the prosecutor compared the funding he finally received to "trying to extinguish a forest fire by spitting on it" (Reed and Cummings 1995). In the final analysis, in terms of the investigation into the events at the Mena airport, the state really did have "next to nothing to do with it."

> On the subject of drug running to fund the Contras, Senator John Kerry said,
>
> Were there Contras who relied on the profits of narcotics in order to buy arms and survive? Yes, I am convinced of that. Once you open up a clandestine network which has the ability to deliver weapons or other goods from this country, leaving airfields secretly under the sanction of a covert operation with public officials, DEA, Customs, law enforcement, whatever, pulled back because of the covert sanctioning, you've opened up the pipeline for nefarious types who are often involved in these kinds of activities to become the people who bring things back in (Moyers 1988).

In other words, we became covertly totalitarianistic in an alleged attempt to fight overt totalitarianism. We became drug-dealing Marxists in an alleged attempt to fight Marxism. We compromised our own national security through proliferating drugs on the streets of the United States to allegedly protect our national security.

What truly makes me angry is the knowledge that African-American and poor communities were targeted for the distribution of these Iran/Contra drugs. As former Assistant Secretary of Housing and Urban Development Catherine Austin Fitts told me, at that time, HUD was being used to "provide geo-coded information to the CIA on communities targeted for drug distribution" (Fitts 2004).

To this day, no one was ever indicted for violating the Boland Amendment. The Reagan administration believed it to be an unconstitutional interference with the President's ability to conduct foreign policy. Congress clearly did not want the CIA funding the Marxist provisional junta called the Contras, so they added the Boland Amendment to stop it. The Reagan administration argued that it only applied to U.S. intelligence agencies, not the National Security Council. Therefore, the rationale said that if Congress would not provide funding, we will sell drugs, arms, or anything else to get the funding to back the Contras.

The question as to whether or not Boland covered the NSC still remains officially unsettled. In my personal opinion, I believe the spirit of what the amendment attempted to accomplish was, indeed, violated.

Nonetheless, in spite of his public pledge not to deal with terrorists and in spite of lying to the American people repeatedly about his involvement, Reagan approved a secret deal allowing Vice Admiral John M. Poindexter and his deputy, Colonel Oliver North, to secretly provide the Nicaraguan Contras with millions of dollars in both taxpayer funds and in proceeds from the sale of drugs in African-American communities in the United States. The President of the United States authorized the sale of missiles to Iran.

Keep in mind, this was the same Khomenite regime in Iran who held Americans as hostages for 444 days. It was the same Khomenite regime in Iran who burned American flags in their streets and shouted "Death to America."

Yes, in spite of the fact that Iran was, and still is, a sworn enemy of the United States, President Reagan violated the public trust, the will of Congress, the Constitution, and compromised this nation's character and security to support them. As Senator John Kerry said,

> They were willing to literally put the Constitution at risk because they believed somehow there was a higher order of things, that the ends are justified by the means. That's the most Marxist thing I ever heard of in my life. If you can have a retired general and a colonel, you know, in mufti, running around, making deals in other countries on their own, soliciting funds to overthrow governments and hide it from the American people so you have no accountability, you've done the very thing that James Madison and the others feared most when they were struggling to put the Constitution together, which was to create an accountable system which didn't have runaway power in one hand so that you could have one person making

a decision and running off against the will of the American people (Moyers 1988).

During the Iran/Contra hearings, House Chief Council John Nields asked Colonel Oliver North, "We do live in a democracy, don't we?"

Colonel North responded, "We do, sir, thank God."

Mr. Nields then asked, "Is it the people, not one Marine Lieutenant Colonel, that get to decide the important policy decisions for the nation?"

North paused for a pregnant moment, and then answered, "Yes" (Moyers 1988).

How can we honor men in uniform and in public office who openly manifest contempt for the public pledges they make to defend the Constitution and secretly work to trash it? Oliver North openly admitted lying to the Congress, and he is treated like a star today. In the hearings, he told Mr. Nields, "I will tell you right now, Counsel, and all the members here gathered, that I misled the Congress" (Moyers 1988). Democrats wanted to prosecute Colonel North for his role.

The final report published after the hearings blamed Reagan's passive style of leadership for allowing the conduct of foreign policy without involvement of any elected official. Nevertheless, Congress allowed $300 million of the taxpayers' hard-earned money to flow to the Contras, only to see the Sandinistas voted out in 1990. The Contra war, which lasted until 1988, resulted in more than 25,000 deaths and 700,000 refugees and displaced people.

There were many more individuals involved, many more lies told, and many more Americans disillusioned with Washington and the notion of civic involvement in government making a difference. I'll just name a few, like Lieutenant Colonel Robert Carl "Bud" McFarlane, Reagan's National Security Advisor from 1983–1986. When McFarlane was State Department counselor in early 1981, he wrote a report called "Taking the War to Nicaragua" that really summed up the Reagan administration's strategy in Central America. That report contained his suggestions to the President on how to do his end-run around Congress, provide support for the Contras, and secure the release of U.S. hostages. His ideas were enacted through the Restricted Inter-Agency Group (RIG) against the admonitions of ranking officials in the White House. Some of those who didn't approve of McFarlane's plans were Secretary of Defense Caspar Weinberger and Secretary of State George Schultz.

As soon as McFarlane retired in May of 1986, planeloads of weapon parts started being flown to the Iranians, with McFarlane as the special envoy. After the first planeload was delivered, Iran still would not cooperate and help secure the release of the hostages held in Lebanon by Hezbollah. In fact, the Iranians went to the press about it. They told the story in detail to the Lebanese weekly magazine, Al Shiraa, about how top Iranian officials refused the quid pro quo. The stuff hit the fan.

The administration was now in damage-control mode. Everyone on the inside knew that the "stuff" would have to roll downhill, and it did.

At that point, White House Chief of Staff Donald Regan went to work spinning the story. McFarlane would have to be one of the fall guys. Still loyal to the President, McFarlane was probably told to just keep quiet because he refused to speak to the press.

Nevertheless, Chief of Staff Regan's accusation that he did the weapons transfers on his own was scaring the hell out of him. Defending himself against Regan making him the fall guy, McFarlane threatened Poindexter with a libel suit.

Like a moth that flew too close to the flame, McFarlane was betrayed by his colleagues and tried to kill himself with an overdose of Valium on February 9, 1987. He ended up pleading guilty in 1988 to four counts of withholding information from Congress for his role in the Iran/Contra cover-up. The court gave him two years probation and a $20,000 fine.

But like Dick Nixon, he and all the other key players in the scandal received a presidential pardon by another Republican President, George H.W. Bush. It was one of the last things Bush did before handing over the White House to Bill Clinton.

I've already mentioned Admiral John Poindexter, who followed McFarlane as National Security Advisor and was also deeply involved with Colonel North in carrying on McFarlane's schemes in both the Iranian and Nicaraguan sides of the scandal.

There were also men like General Richard Secord who flew 285 combat missions while serving in Southeast Asia during the 1960s. He helped the CIA with its secret war in Laos. From 1975 to 1978, he was chief of the Air Force section of the U.S. Military Assistance Advisory Group, which sold weapons to the Shah of Iran. It was at that time that he met Albert Hakim, who would later become his business partner in the Enterprise. Secord was promoted to major general in May 1980, and was the ranking Air Force officer in charge of rescue efforts for U.S. hostages held in Iran during 1980–81. After serving as deputy assistant secretary of Defense for International Security Affairs from 1981 to 1983, he retired from the Air Force following allegations of improper dealings with former CIA agent Edwin Wilson, who was convicted of smuggling arms to Libya.

There were others involved on many different levels as well. The history is well documented. Hopefully, I have given the reader enough background on the Iran/Contra Affair to conclude how far this nation was taken into darkness in the name of national security.

The Iran/Contra Affair is significant because America still faces today the questions it brought into public view two decades ago. Does the President have unilateral authority to conduct private and unlawful foreign policy in the name of national security? Can the President sell arms to a foreign nation without congressional approval? What information does the President have to disclose to Congress and when? Does the President have to include the Congress in foreign policy? Does Congress have the right to oversee the covert actions of the White House? Does the President have to get approval from the Congress on funding for covert operations? Who regulates and controls that kind of budgeting? Can the

Supreme Court decide and settle conflicts between the Congress and the White House? How far can America go in support of armed opposition forces seeking to overthrow a government?

These constitutional and ethical questions are still unresolved. Will there ever be a legal remedy if the legislative and executive branches do not wish to work together? The biggest question of all is — how much of the Constitution are we willing to sacrifice in the name of national security?

Chronology of Key Public Events

- Oct. 5, 1986: Nicaraguan soldiers shoot down a Contra resupply plane; Eugene Hasenfus, an American, survives.

- Nov. 3, 1986: Lebanese newspaper Al-Shiraa reports that the United States secretly sold arms to Iran.

- Nov. 6, 1986: President Reagan denies arms were sold to Iran.

- Nov. 13, 1986: President Reagan acknowledges weapons were sold to Iran, but denies that the arms were sold to win the release of American hostages.

- Nov. 19, 1986: President Reagan holds a news conference at which he denies U.S. involvement in shipments prior to January 1986.

- Nov. 25, 1986: White House discloses Contra diversion from the Iran arms sales.

- Dec. 1, 1986: Tower Commission appointed by President Reagan.

- Dec. 4, 1986: Meese requests appointment of Independent Counsel on Iran/Contra.

- Dec. 6, 1986: Swiss financial records of Enterprise requested by Department of Justice pursuant to treaty.

- Dec. 19, 1986: Walsh appointed Independent Counsel.

- Jan. 6, 1987: Senate creates Iran/Contra committee.

- Jan. 7, 1987: House creates Iran/Contra committee.

- Jan. 29, 1987: Senate Select Committee on Intelligence issues report on Iran/Contra.

- Feb. 7, 1987: Swiss Office for Police Matters approves request for financial records; Albert Hakim and Manucher Ghorbanifar appeal.

- Feb. 26, 1987: Tower Commission issues Iran/Contra report.

- March 5, 1987: Walsh receives parallel appointment as Independent Counsel from Justice Department.

- March 18, 1987: Walsh reaches agreement with House and Senate Iran/Contra committees to delay voting on and obtaining immunized testimony by North and Poindexter.

- April 28, 1987: Independent Counsel submits First Interim Report to Congress on potential problems caused by immunity grants.

- April 29, 1987: Carl "Spitz" Channell pleads guilty to conspiracy to defraud the United States.

- May 5, 1987: Congress begins public hearings on Iran/Contra.

- May 6, 1987: Richard R. Miller pleads guilty to conspiracy to defraud the United States.

- July 7–10 and July 13–14, 1987: North testifies publicly under grant of immunity before Congress.

- July 15–17 and July 20–21, 1987: Poindexter testifies publicly under grant of immunity before Congress.

- Nov. 10, 1987: Swiss financial records of Enterprise received by Independent Counsel.

- Nov. 18, 1987: Congress issues Iran/Contra report.

- Jan. 22, 1988: The U.S. Court of Appeals for the District of Columbia strikes down the Independent Counsel Law as unconstitutional.

- March 11, 1988: McFarlane pleads guilty to withholding information from Congress.

- March 16, 1988: North, Poindexter, Secord, and Hakim indicted on conspiracy to defraud the United States and other charges.

- June 8, 1988: Judge Gesell orders separate trials for North, Poindexter, Secord, and Hakim due to problems caused by congressional grants of immunity.

- June 20, 1988: Fernandez indicted in District of Columbia for conspiracy and false statements to the CIA Inspector General and the Tower Commission.

- June 29, 1988: Supreme Court upholds the constitutionality of the Independent Counsel Law.

- Oct. 19, 1988: Judge Robinson dismisses Fernandez case without prejudice on venue grounds.

- Jan. 13, 1989: Central conspiracy and theft charges against North are dismissed because of classified information problems.

- Jan. 31, 1989 to May 4, 1989: North trial resulting in three-count conviction.

- April 7, 1989: Secord is indicted on nine additional charges of obstruction, false statements, and perjury.

- April 21, 1989: Fernandez indicted on false statement and obstruction charges in eastern district of Virginia.

- July 24, 1989: Attorney general obtains a stay of the Fernandez trial to appeal Classified Information Procedures Act (CIPA) rulings.

- Aug. 23, 1989: The Fourth Circuit U.S. Court of Appeals hears oral arguments in Fernandez on the attorney general's right to appeal under CIPA.

- Sept. 19, 1989: Walsh testifies before the legislative subcommittee of the House Permanent Select Committee on Intelligence on CIPA and submits a report to the House and Senate judiciary committees and the Senate Intelligence Committee.

- Sept. 29, 1989: The Fourth Circuit rules that the attorney general does not have standing under CIPA to appeal trial court rulings in cases prosecuted by Independent Counsel. It dismisses the appeal and remands the case to the district court.

- Nov. 8, 1989: Secord pleads guilty to making false statements to Congress.

- Nov. 21, 1989: Hakim pleads guilty to illegally supplementing the salary of a government official; Lake Resources Inc. pleads guilty to a corporate felony of diverting Iran arms sales proceeds to the Contras.

- Nov. 24, 1989: Fernandez is dismissed after the attorney general refuses to allow the disclosure of certain classified information at trial. Independent Counsel files notice with the Fourth Circuit U.S. Court of Appeals that the government will appeal the trial court's CIPA rulings.

- Dec. 11, 1989: Independent Counsel submits Second Interim Report to Congress on CIPA.

- Dec. 12, 1989: Walsh testifies on CIPA in closed session of the legislative subcommittee of the House Intelligence Committee.

- Feb. 6, 1990: North appeal oral arguments.

- Feb. 16–17, 1990: Reagan gives videotaped deposition on Poindexter.

- Feb. 22, 1990: Thomas G. Clines is indicted on tax charges.

- Feb. 22, 1990: Walsh testifies on CIPA in a closed session of the Senate Intelligence Committee.

- March 5, 1990 to April 7, 1990: Poindexter trial, resulting in five-count conviction.

- Sept. 6, 1990: Fourth U.S. Circuit Court of Appeals upholds trial court's rulings on Fernandez.

- Sept. 4–18, 1990: Clines trial, resulting in convictions on four felony charges.

- Oct. 12, 1990: Fernandez dismissed after attorney general notifies trial court that he has made a final determination not to withdraw CIPA 6(e) affidavit to bar use of classified information.

- Oct. 24–25, 1990: Walsh reports to the Congressional Intelligence and Judiciary committees on final outcome of Fernandez.

- May 28, 1991: Supreme Court declines review of North case.

- July 9, 1991: Alan D. Fiers Jr. pleads guilty to withholding information from Congress.

- Sept. 6, 1991: Clair E. George is indicted on 10 counts of perjury, false statements, and obstruction.

- Sept. 16, 1991: Case against North is dismissed on motion of Independent Counsel after two days of hearings by the trial court.

- Oct. 7, 1991: Elliott Abrams pleads guilty to withholding information from Congress.

- Nov. 15, 1991: U.S. Court of Appeals for the District of Columbia Circuit reverses Poindexter's convictions.

- Nov. 26, 1991: Duane R. Clarridge is indicted on seven counts of perjury and false statements.

- Feb. 27, 1992: Fourth Circuit U.S. Court of Appeals affirms Clines' convictions.

- May 21, 1992: Clair George is reindicted on two additional charges after three are dismissed with Independent Counsel's consent; George now faces nine felony charges.

- May 25, 1992: Thomas Clines begins serving 16-month jail sentence.

- June 16, 1992: Former Defense Secretary Caspar W. Weinberger is indicted on five felony charges of obstruction, perjury, and false statements in Congressional and Independent Council investigations.

- June 24, 1992: Walsh issues Third Interim Report to Congress, stating that investigation is in its final phase and focusing on whether high-ranking administration officials beginning in November 1986 tried to obstruct official investigations into the 1985 Iran arms sales.

- July 13, 1992: George trial begins.

- August 26, 1992: Mistrial declared in George case after jury fails to reach a verdict. Independent Counsel announces that the case will be retried.

- Sept. 17, 1992: Walsh informs Chief Judge George MacKinnon of the Independent Counsel appointing panel and Attorney General William

Barr that the investigation is complete barring unforeseen developments at the remaining trials.

- Sept. 29, 1992: Judge Hogan dismisses Count 1, an obstruction of Congress charge, in the Weinberger case on grounds it does not conform to the Poindexter appeals ruling on the obstruction statute.

- Oct. 19, 1992: George retrial on seven counts begins.

- Oct. 30, 1992: Weinberger is reindicted on a false statement charge, replacing the previously dismissed Count 1 obstruction charge.

- Dec. 7, 1992: Supreme Court declines to review Poindexter.

- Dec. 9, 1992: George is found guilty on two counts of false statements and perjury before Congress; sentencing is set for February 1993.

- Dec. 11, 1992: Judge Hogan dismisses the new one-count indictment against Weinberger on statute of limitations grounds, leaving four charges remaining.

- Dec. 11, 1992: White House informs Independent Counsel that President Bush has kept diaries relevant to Iran/Contra, which have never been produced to investigators.

- Dec. 24, 1992: President Bush pardons Weinberger, Clarridge, McFarlane, Fiers, Abrams, and George. Independent Counsel denounces pardons.

- Jan. 5, 1993: Weinberger trial was scheduled to begin.

- Feb. 8, 1993: Independent Council issues Fourth Interim Report to Congress on the Weinberger case and the Presidential pardons (Chronology of Key Public Events).

Chapter Eight

★ ★ ★ ★ ★

The War on Terror

The Lessons of 911

Much has been written on the events of September 11, 2001. The subject has become a cottage industry in America. There have been numerous videos, books, papers, magazine articles, conferences, shows, and Web sites on the subject. Therefore, I wish not to belabor the issue except to mention a few points on how a protracted war such as Bush's so-called war on terror provides the perfect political atmosphere to advance various hegemonic policies in the name of national security. How we react to the threat of terrorism will forever change and reshape America.

Indeed, President Bush has said that 911 changed everything for him. The lesson he claims to have learned is that the great oceans can no longer protect us. Therefore, in fulfilling his duty as President to answer 911's wake-up call, he has been forced to implement sweeping, unilateral, executive actions. Since it is his sworn duty is to protect the U.S., his conclusion is that we must proactively fight terrorism and countries that support terrorists to prevent this from ever happening again. Most conservatives feel this justifies the Bush administration's doctrinal shift toward the preemptive and unilateral military action currently underway in Iraq. President Bush has also gone so far as to label Iraq, Iran, and North Korea an "Axis of Evil" (Bush 2002).

In the psychological fog of that fateful day in September of 2001, most Americans rallied around the President. In that evening's 8:30 p.m. EST address, his words seemed to comfort and inspire a stunned nation.

> Good evening. Today, our fellow citizens, our way of life, our very freedom came under attack in a series of deliberate and deadly terrorist acts. The victims were in airplanes, or in their offices; secretaries, businessmen and women, military and federal workers; moms and dads, friends and neighbors. Thousands of lives were suddenly ended by evil, despicable acts of terror.

> The pictures of airplanes flying into buildings, fires burning, huge structures collapsing, have filled us with disbelief, terrible sadness, and a quiet, unyielding anger. These acts of mass murder were intended to frighten our nation into chaos and retreat. But they have failed; our country is strong.

A great people have been moved to defend a great nation. Terrorist attacks can shake the foundations of our biggest buildings, but they cannot touch the foundation of America. These acts shattered steel, but they cannot dent the steel of American resolve. America was targeted for attack because we're the brightest beacon for freedom and opportunity in the world. And no one will keep that light from shining.

Today, our nation saw evil, the very worst of human nature. And we responded with the best of America — with the daring of our rescue workers, with the caring for strangers and neighbors who came to give blood and help in any way they could. Immediately following the first attack, I implemented our government's emergency response plans. Our military is powerful, and it's prepared. Our emergency teams are working in New York City and Washington, D.C. to help with local rescue efforts. Our first priority is to get help to those who have been injured and to take every precaution to protect our citizens at home and around the world from further attacks.

The functions of our government continue without interruption. Federal agencies in Washington which had to be evacuated today are reopening with essential personnel tonight and will be open for business tomorrow. Our financial institutions remain strong, and the American economy will be open for business, as well.

The search is underway for those who are behind these evil acts. I've directed the full resources of our intelligence and law enforcement communities to find those responsible and to bring them to justice. We will make no distinction between the terrorists who committed these acts and those who harbor them.

I appreciate so very much the members of Congress who have joined me in strongly condemning these attacks. And on behalf of the American people, I thank the many world leaders who have called to offer their condolences and assistance. America and our friends and allies join with all those who want peace and security in the world, and we stand together to win the war against terrorism. Tonight, I ask for your prayers for all those who grieve, for the children whose worlds have been shattered, for all whose sense of safety and security has been threatened. And I pray they will be comforted by a power greater than any of us, spoken through the ages in Psalm 23: "Even though I walk through the valley of the shadow of death, I fear no evil, for You are with me."

This is a day when all Americans from every walk of life unite in our resolve for justice and peace. America has stood down enemies before, and we will do so this time. None of us will ever forget this day. Yet, we go forward to defend freedom and all that is good and just in our world. Thank you. Good night, and God bless America (Bush 2001).

It's amazing how great a distance we have moved from the goodwill of the world since that evening. Well wishes and pledges of support were showered on America from all over the world, including the Middle East. Today, unfortunately for all of us, the Bush administration's response in dealing with the threat of global, stateless terrorism has made America a global pariah. He has completely misinterpreted "the lessons of 911." If we want to prevent another disaster like that, we should consider some of the key points and obvious lessons that the attacks of 911 illuminated.

Disarmament of Confrontational Foreign Powers

Disarmament of foreign powers alone is an insufficient tactical response to assure our national security. Why? Because our own weapons, as well as improvised weaponry, are too easily accessible and can easily be used by anyone to attack us. The fact that commercial passenger planes were allegedly commandeered by Islamic radicals and used as missiles to perpetrate the attacks of 911 proves that terrorists do not need to purchase any weapons of any kind from any foreign power. Those sick individuals who planned and carried out the attacks of 911 proved that materials that can be readily obtained in the U.S. can be used to kill thousands, and maybe millions, of innocent people.

Therefore, the U.S. cannot prevent such attacks by disarming Iraq, the Axis of Evil, or any other country. Even if we disarmed every single country in the world, it would not have prevented 911 because terrorists can make ample use of just about anything as a weapon of mass destruction.

Hospitals contain enough radiological material to fashion a dirty bomb. Trains routinely carrying hazardous materials in virtually every city in this country can easily be sabotaged and create devastation. In fact, a visit to the local hardware store can provide enough fertilizer, resin, pesticides, and other common materials for any individual evil enough to create havoc in this country. So disarmament of foreign powers, hostile or otherwise, is not a credible total solution to this new stateless threat.

So what will it take to truly keep us safe? It will take the help of intelligence agencies all over the world, working together to protect the lives of the innocent. It will take strengthening those international treaties that worked to save the world from thermonuclear destruction during the Cold War. It will take strengthening and expanding the Transatlantic Alliance in a new, cooperative initiative for peace. It will take a concentrated effort at diplomatic engagement for those regimes in the process of transforming themselves from purveyors of terror to join the world community of nations seeking peace. It will take paying attention to the concerns of those nations so long afflicted by the Washington Consensus and begin anew to address the negative aspects of the free market within their countries. It will take a carefully crafted program of incentives and sanctions to prod those regimes away from developing weapons of mass destruction in favor of substantive trade agreements and development assistance. Peaceful nations must work to strengthen those elements within hostile regimes that seek economic development, giving them the leverage to succeed in their struggle against the hawks in their societies. It will take seeking profit in peace instead of war. All we need is the will of mankind to overcome fear, anxiety, and aggression, which will free our souls to pursue a just and lasting peace for our children.

Homeland Security Bureaucracy

President George W. Bush created the Department of Homeland Security, the most significant transformation and expansion of the U.S. government in over a half-century. The White House concluded that by transforming and realigning the current confusing patchwork of government activities into a single department, it would better enable the President to fulfill his primary mission, which is to protect our homeland. The creation of a Department of Homeland Security (DHS), we were told, is one more key step in the President's national strategy for homeland security. But is merely increasing the government's bureaucracy, in an attempt to streamline it, sufficient to cover the gaps in this nation's security net?

The ominous specter of "weapons of mass destruction" is not the only threat for which the DHS has been tasked to respond. The naturally occurring incidents of mass destruction, or more accurately, "incidents of national significance," (Emergencies and Response: Emphasis on Local Response 2002) like the recent hurricanes that destroyed much of the Gulf Coast and Florida, has shown us some of the inability of this new bureaucracy in fulfilling its stated objectives.

After Hurricane Katrina turned parts of New Orleans into an extension of Lake Pontchartrain, the conservative pundits in the media tried to blame local and state officials for the slow response in recovery and disaster relief. But when you visit the Office of Homeland Security's Web site and read its response plan for emergencies and disasters, you'll find it plainly states,

> All incidents are handled at the lowest possible organizational and jurisdictional level. Police, fire, public health and medical, emergency management, and other personnel are responsible for incident management at the local level. For those events that rise to the level of an Incident of National Significance, the Department of Homeland Security provides operational and/or resource coordination for Federal support to on-scene incident command structures (Emergencies and Response: Emphasis on Local Response 2002).

But where was the federal government after Hurricane Katrina blew through? Where was FEMA? Where was the Office of Homeland Security? The thousands of residents in New Orleans and other areas affected by Katrina are living and breathing testimonies to just a few of the many holes in the system that this recent expansion of government has failed to plug.

In response to when a terrorist threat is revealed by our intelligence apparatus, we increase security measures. But it seems no matter how many times we increase our security measures, we find additional holes in the safety net. Security was beefed up in the wake of the attacks of September 11, 2001, yet incidents still occur in the air and airport security is still breached on the ground. Since that time, security experiments by local law enforcement agencies illustrated time and time again how easily airport security can be breached.

National security experts are well aware that terrorists know where the security weaknesses are and how to exploit them. They are well aware of the fact that simply increasing security is not a sufficient solution to this new threat. As Osama bin Laden, himself, said on a tape aired by Al-Jazeera on January 19, 2006,

> ... the mujahideen holy warriors, with God's grace, have managed repeatedly to penetrate all security measures adopted by the unjust allied countries. The proof of that is the explosions you have seen in the capitals of the European nations who are in this aggressive coalition. The delay in similar operations happening in America has not been because of failure to break through your security measures. The operations are under preparation and you will see them in your homes the minute they are through with preparations, with God's permission (Osama bin Laden 2006).

In the final analysis, we can create as many new bureaucracies as we want, but a free society such as ours is nearly impossible to completely shield from terrorist attacks. The ideology of free market corporate liberalism demands our borders remain as porous as Swiss cheese.

In search of cheap labor, capitalism accepts the risk of allowing people with malicious intent to routinely enter the United States carrying lawful visas. The fact of the matter is that the United States has the most open immigration policy of any industrialized nation on earth, except with regards to Haitians. A cover story in E-Magazine entitled, "Balancing Act: Can America Sustain a Population of 500 Million — Or Even a Billion — by 2100?" tells us,

> A 1993 Hispanic USA Research Group survey showed that 89% of Hispanic Americans strongly support an immediate moratorium on immigration, and 74% feel fewer immigrants should be allowed and stronger restrictions should be enforced. But business groups still lobby for an open door immigration policy to suppress the high wages that would otherwise be demanded in a full-employment economy, and there is no comparable countervailing pressure. And politicians support high immigration levels for fear of alienating large ethnic voting blocks (Cabib 2000).

Like Indiana Jones seeking some lost treasure and accepting great peril associated with its acquisition in the process, so has business in America and their poodles in government placed us all at risk for an increasingly hard-to-find treasure.

Improper Targeting

If terrorism is a stateless threat, then it is impossible to defeat terrorists by way of an exclusively state-based military campaign. In other words, since terrorists are hiding all over the world, why would you focus and confine most of your tactical measures to one country? The alleged perpetrators of 911 were from nations that are supposed to be friendly to the United States. Osama bin Laden and 15 of the 19 alleged hijackers were from Saudi Arabia. The others were from Egypt.

Yet these countries say they are our friends and have claimed to have no association with al-Qaeda. I believe that if Saudi Arabia is truly a friend to the people of the United States, they sure do have a strange way of showing it. Allow me to explain why.

Although the Saudis have been considered our allies for decades and have received diplomatic engagement from our presidents since 1945, doubts have now arisen about their loyalty in some quarters. Indeed, the way in which some of our presidents (especially both G. W. Bush and G. H. W. Bush) have fawned over the Saudis has been questioned and even condemned by many people in this country.

Daniel Pipes of the Council on Foreign Relations has harshly criticized Washington's engagement of the Saudi regime in an article entitled "The Scandal of U.S./Saudi Relations." In that article, Pipes describes how a "culture of corruption in the Executive Branch renders it quite incapable of dealing with the Kingdom of Saudi Arabia in the farsighted and disinterested manner that U.S. foreign policy requires" (Pipes 2002/03).

Mohammed Al-Khilewi, a Saudi diplomat who defected to the United States, was quoted in a statement by Patricia M. Roush before the Committee on Government Reform, U.S. House of Representatives. Al-Khilewi said, "When it comes to the Saudi-American relationship, the White House should be called the White Tent" (Roush 2002).

There are indications that the Saudis are both with us and against us, playing both ends against the middle in an effort to preserve their kingdom. That is to say, the Saudis profess to be our allies and have helped us at crucial times, just as we have stood by them, notably when Saddam Hussein had them in his sights 12 years ago.

However, the Saudis also reportedly lend support to some of our worst enemies. The Saudi rulers operate an oppressive and dictatorial regime. They have historically demonstrated a willingness to do business with terrorists, or with anyone else, to preserve their kingdom.

They are happy Saddam is gone, but I wonder how happy they are seeing a democracy develop in nearby Iraq. I'm sure they wouldn't like their subjects getting any ideas or becoming inspired to emulate the emerging political dynamics of Iraq.

Let's examine a few points: Saudi Arabia has dibbled and dabbled in support of terrorism, they helped to sponsor an OPEC oil embargo of the U.S. when U.S. and Soviet tensions nearly led to naval conflict in the Mediterranean in the early 1970s, and their view of Middle East democratization is parasympathetic.

In a newspaper article entitled "Briefing Depicted Saudis as Enemies," Laurent Murawiec, a Rand Corp. analyst said, "The Saudis are active at every level of the terror chain, from planners to financiers, from cadre to foot-soldier, from ideologist to cheerleader. Saudi Arabia supports our enemies and attacks our allies" (Murawiec 2002).

This was an explosive briefing. It was presented on July 10 to the Defense Policy Board, a group of prominent intellectuals and former senior officials that advises the Pentagon on defense policy. Yet the United States continues to maintain that its official policy is not to make deals with terrorists.

Consider also the question of security and counter-proliferation of nuclear, biological, and chemical weapons-related materials. In an article entitled "Can Bush or Kerry Prevent Nuclear Terrorism?" Charles D. Ferguson of the Arms Control Association concluded that terrorists have essentially four mechanisms by which they can exploit military and civilian nuclear assets around the world to serve their destructive ends.

First, according to Ferguson, there is the threat of "the seizure and detonation of an intact nuclear weapon" (Ferguson 2004). In my opinion, this is an unlikely scenario. Simply because, according to many experts in the field, unless it is a dirty bomb, which is far less complicated to handle, the level of logistical capability of handling, transporting, and detonating a fully operational nuclear warhead or bomb exceeds the reach of today's stateless terrorist organizations.

If that kind of device is ever used anywhere in the world, the most likely perpetrator would be a military organization tied to some rogue government. According to Joseph Cirincione, director for the Carnegie Endowment for International Peace's program on nonproliferation,

> A terrorist group, no matter how determined or
> how well funded, could not make the nuclear

material for a bomb by itself. Instead, terrorists would have to steal the material or a nuclear weapon — most likely from the stockpiles of smaller, tactical nuclear weapons in Russia or from Pakistan's nuclear arsenal. Furthermore, a terrorist attack with a radiological dispersal device (RDD), or dirty bomb, is more feasible than a nuclear terrorist strike, since the device itself is easier to assemble and the sources are more available than the HEU [highly enriched uranium] or plutonium needed for a nuclear bomb (Lehrer 2005).

Second, according to Ferguson, there is a possibility of the "theft or purchase of highly enriched uranium (HEU) or plutonium, leading to the fabrication and detonation of a crude nuclear weapon or an improvised nuclear device (IND)" (Ferguson 2004).

Again, elements like highly enriched uranium and plutonium 235 are so hazardous that I question whether or not they could be developed into a bomb, deployed, and actually detonated before the terrorists handling it would die or become too incapacitated from exposure to it. Suitcase nukes are quite simply the stuff of movies.

Third, according to Ferguson, there is the possibility of "attacks against and sabotage of nuclear facilities, such as nuclear power plants, to try to cause the release of large amounts of radioactivity" (Ferguson 2004).

This is a far more likely scenario because of the security vulnerability of current nuclear power facilities in America. Items such as shoulder-fired missiles are readily available on the black market and could be used to breach containment-related facilities, possibly creating a meltdown.

Fourth, Ferguson points to an area that I have already indicated. That is "the unauthorized acquisition of radioactive materials contributing to the construction and detonation of a radiological dispersion device, popularly known as a dirty bomb or a radiation emission device" (Ferguson 2004).

I strongly believe Ferguson is right in being concerned about the proliferation of fissile materials. Promises have been made by our leaders to control the situation; however, not enough is being done. Since the collapse of the Soviet Union, there are still some 600 metric tons of fissile material in Russia that many experts and political leaders feel is not sufficiently secured. Senator John Kerry spoke about this potential threat to American national security interests many times during his 2004 presidential campaign.

During the campaign, the Bush administration, which largely ignored the issue prior to Senator Kerry's raising it and pledging to do something about it if he were elected, had Secretary of Energy Spencer Abraham vow on July 17, 2004, one month after the publication of the Kerry plan, that his department will finish securing 600 metric tons of weapons-usable material in Russia by 2008.

Today, the Russians are supposed to be our friends. Yet there has been a resistance towards verification of the security measures within Russia as it pertains to this potential threat. But President Bush fawns over President Putin as if there were no problem at all.

Does our President have the diplomatic leverage to deal with this issue? This is the question I pose. This is a major area of concern to people like Dr. Zbigniew Brzezinski, his son Mark, myself, and others who are knowledgeable of this area of Eurasian affairs. Dr. Brzezinski has been a staunch critic of the Bush administration's handling of this issue, and I agree with him 100 percent.

These points clearly illustrate why attacking governments who we believe are confrontational is not a sufficient solution to this new threat of terrorism. With friends like these, who needs enemies?

The truth is, governments of unfriendly nations are not the only problem; the so-called friendly nations are dangerous too. Even if America completely obliterated every unfriendly government today, attacks like 911 can still happen tomorrow.

Also, don't forget that American professionals trained the alleged terrorists in the United States to fly the passenger jets they used as weapons of mass destruction, all under the watchful apparatus of our national security state.

Our Foreign Petroleum Overdependence

Simply put, America is far too dependent on foreign oil. To go a step further, our petroleum-based economy, from the working-class perspective, is not only out of step with the advances of technology, it is destroying our way of life.

The internal combustion engine has been obsolete for over 70 years, yet the Republican-controlled Congress and the President have steadfastly refused to force automobile manufacturers to significantly increase mileage and fuel efficiency standards through improved patented technology in carburetors and fuel injection systems for cars in America.

Instead, our automobile manufacturers are allowed to keep building cars lighter to improve fuel efficiency, putting us all at greater risk of catastrophic injury or death on the highway.

There are patented carburetors and injection systems capable of producing over 100 MPG. Why are they not brought to the market? Not only that, it has taken far too long to develop hybrid technology for cars and light trucks in America.

Is our government incapable of providing some economic relief to our overburdened petroleum-addicted society? Let us not mention the fact that 911 should have shown us the folly of subsidizing attacks on our own country with money we are spending on foreign oil. Yes, sometimes that money finds its way into the coffers of terrorists.

Finally, the competition among industrialized nations for control and access to the dwindling oil reserves on this planet, particularly in nations that are already highly unstable, is exceedingly dangerous. According to the Jamestown Foundation, a nonpartisan think tank (specializing in Eurasian affairs, terrorism, events, and trends in those societies which are strategically or tactically important to the United States), frequently, the foundation restricts access to such information, but now it is publicly pointing out how America's "sphere of influence" in Latin America is being encroached upon by China. In an article for the foundation by Chietigj Bajpaee entitled "Chinese Energy Strategy in Latin America," the author states,

> Latin America is fast emerging as the major stage of competition for oil and gas resources among the global powers. The region, which has traditionally come under the U.S. sphere of influence, caught the attention of China following the significant growth potential of its energy resources. Latin America is estimated to hold 13.5 percent of the world's proven oil reserves, but accounts for only 6 percent of total output. Although China has tapped energy resources in Venezuela, Columbia, Ecuador, and Peru, and has begun to tap Argentina and Bolivia, there still exists significant room for expansion, especially given that China still depends on the Middle East for 60 percent of its oil imports and wishes to further diversify (Chietigj Bajpaee 2005).

Given the fact of the recent solidarity among populist Latin American leaders who are increasingly viewed by Washington as becoming more confrontational, and China's recent activity in the area of resource merger and acquisition, increased preferential trade agreements, and control of the Panama Canal, Washington has a serious problem on its hands. The dragon is hungry, and it is feeding in our backyard. My prayer is that we won't have a fight between our two powerful nations, like two big dogs trying to eat from the same bowl. Today, one must wonder if the Monroe Doctrine can survive globalism.

But not only does this powder keg exist in Latin America, the same avaricious competition for oil exists in other volatile areas of the globe in Central Europe, West Africa, and the Middle East. For these, and many other reasons, I strongly believe that in the post-911 world, it is essential that the U.S. include in its foreign policy agenda a way to curtail dependence on foreign oil.

Why Do They Hate Us?

After 911, it seemed like every night on the news, we were told that radical Islamic fundamentalists hate us because they are jealous of us. If you believe that, then I have the proverbial swampland to sell you.

Quite frankly, it makes me angry that the media thinks we are that stupid. I do not believe in talking down to the American people. I think we are a lot smarter than the mainstream media that too often tries to dumb us down thinks we are.

The truth is, anti-Americanism is caused by many factors. But the root cause of it in the Middle East is religious in nature, as well as geopolitical. For one thing, they despise our support of Israel. Those factions in the Middle East who would love to see more events like 911 happen to America often feel that way because of our hegemonic foreign policies.

If we want to stop the attacks, we must address the root causes. The American people are too often listening to the talking heads, but should hear more from experts on Osama bin Laden like Milton Bearden. Bearden was with the

Central Intelligence Agency from 1964–1994. As its field officer in Afghanistan, he oversaw the CIA's $3 billion covert aid program for Afghan rebels fighting the Soviets. At that time, Osama bin Laden was leading Arab volunteers to fight his "jihad" there.

Mr. Bearden tells us that Osama bin Laden's primary goal has always been to end the U.S. military presence in Saudi Arabia. He also says that the way Osama bin Laden has been cast by the media as the mastermind behind "every known terrorist act in the last decade" (Bearden 2002) is a joke. According to Bearden in a PBS documentary called "Hunting bin Laden,"

> Osama bin Laden has chosen to make himself an enemy of the United States. He has issued these disputable fatwahs, these Islamic proclamations, to kill all ... Americans and Jews. Therefore, he's made himself a component, and I think that the United States is absolutely justified in taking out Osama bin Laden. But to oversimplify it by linking him to every known terrorist act in the last decade is an insult to most Americans. And it certainly doesn't encourage our allies in this to take us very seriously. Osama bin Laden is a legitimate target for the United States, period. But then, to completely reinforce it with all of these insupportable accusations, I think, is a disservice and an oversimplification (Bearden 2002).

But for what other reason does Osama bin Laden hate America? Is it because we are a superpower, or is it because of our harshness toward their people? Bearden stated,

Partly, [because we are a superpower] but we're also a superpower who insists on being perceived by the least fortunate of the Islamic world as being somehow against them. It is not missed in Friday prayers that we sent 75 million dollars worth of missiles flying against the two poorest Islamic countries in the world, Afghanistan and Sudan. I spent too many years living in the shadow of one mosque or another not to take what happens at Friday prayers seriously. And that's what's going on (Bearden 2002).

The plain truth, that seemingly no one in America wants to face, is that since 911, no one likes us any more. Our image has been significantly tarnished in our response to the attacks. We would be foolish to believe it's because they are jealous of us. It is our foreign policies, before, during, and after 911 that has even 87 percent of Europe in a recent Time Europe poll saying that the United States is the "biggest threat to world peace" (Europe News Poll 2003).

The Bush administration has turned our international reputation from bad to worse, and we must act pragmatically to correct it. That means true statesmanship and a kind of internationalism that honors treaties and institutions that work to advance the healing of wounds instead of a plutocratic and hegemonic agenda.

It is dangerous for an open society to be viewed as an enemy or a threat. But at the same time, we must be seen as willing to protect ourselves too. It's a very delicate balance, and one that we must find before it's too late.

Because of this chronic imbalance, the world used to only criticize our leaders. Today, we have allowed our leaders to make the world despise all things American. President Bush is no more likeable than Saddam Hussein in polls in Germany and Austria.

A new poll by the Washington-based Pew Research Center indicates that the number of Europeans with a favorable image of the United States has plummeted, even among the so-called coalition of the willing. In Italy today, only 34 percent view the U.S. positively, compared to 70 percent in 2002. In Spain, only 14 percent have a favorable image. Even in Eastern Europe, support for the U.S. has dropped from 80 percent to 50 percent in Poland.

We are clearly moving in the wrong direction. We are expending a lot of time, money, and resources to make things worse, instead of better.

The Biggest Miscalculation and Blunder since 911

We were told that Osama bin Laden was the mastermind behind the attacks of 911. If this is true and bin Laden is responsible for the deaths of over 3,000 American citizens on U.S. soil, then why has the President not used every resource at his disposal to capture him? When asked about the whereabouts of Osama, why did President Bush say, "You know, I just don't spend that much time on him" (Bush 2002).

To many Americans, that answer was not only way too cavalier, it was callous and unbecoming of a leader on the hunt for the greatest mass murderer in U.S. history. Those words cut like a knife to many of the families who lost loved ones on 911.

But I believe the President was sincere. Why? Because you can make your mouth say anything, but the way that the Bush administration bungled the hunt for bin Laden at Tora Bora in December 2001 speaks louder than words.

Today, no one knows exactly where Osama bin Laden is hiding. What we do know is, at that time (December 2001) and in that place (Tora Bora), we virtually had bin Laden cornered — and we let him get away.

According to American intelligence officials who interrogated captured al-Qaeda fighters and interviewed them separately, Osama bin Laden, a group of top aides, and top members of his elite international 055 Brigade were all trapped in the mountains of Tora Bora in eastern Afghanistan.

Keep in mind, this was winter, and the winter winds in those mountains are very strong, bringing with them a chill that could kill. The Bush administration knew how extremely cold it gets during that time of year, and how many of the established trails that traverse the White Mountains, where Tora Bora is located, are snowed in, making it nearly impossible for man or beast to pass. The Bush administration also knew that this would have limited bin Laden's escape routes and would have given them a better opportunity to intercept and kill him.

According to many accounts, Osama was merely wearing a lightweight camouflage jacket for warmth. He was armed only with a Kalashnikov. In other words, he should have been a sitting duck, and the Bush administration knew it.

The American people need to know that the Afghan locals are not the only people who know those mountains. The CIA financed the Tora Bora bunker complex, with its miles of fully ventilated caves, tunnels, and sophisticated living quarters with electrical generating power systems for the mujahideen during the Afghan/Soviet War.

In addition, the CIA was fully aware of the fact that Osama bin Laden had been very busy renovating Tora Bora just prior to the attacks of 911. Bin Laden brought in tons of heavy construction and land development equipment from the Saudi Bin Laden Group. The Saudi Bin Laden Group is a construction company owned by Osama bin Laden's father.

As a result of the company's status with the U.S., the Saudi Bin Laden Group became one of the most prosperous construction companies in the world. The CIA knew where Bin Laden was, whom he was with, and what he had been doing. Yet they let him get away.

One of the chief CIA covert operatives during Washington's proxy war with the Soviets in Afghanistan was Yunis Khalis. Khalis was very familiar with the U.S. intelligence apparatus; he had been a part of it. However, his loyalty was extremely dubious.

Just like Lenin, who accepted the help of Wall Street during the rise of the Soviet empire, Khalis accepted Washington's money and help against the Soviets. We were using him, and he was using us. The CIA saw in the Afghan alliances a way to once and for all ruin the Soviet Union. So without hesitation, they engaged this dubious leader of one of the most brutal alliances of Afghan resistance groups.

U.S. intelligence knew that they would carry out this proxy campaign with an extreme vengeance. They were well aware of how Khalis and his organization would routinely kill even their own countrymen if they believed they were sympathizers with the Soviets.

As payment, Khalis netted the third-largest share of the more than $3 billion of the CIA's weapons and assistance for his jihad against the Red Army. With the help of the CIA, Khalis became the godfather of Jalalabad, the capital of the province of Nangarhar. He controlled a vast territory which included the strategically indispensable Tora Bora.

But soon the CIA's attack dog was about to turn on his master. What started out as a key operational center for the Mujahideen during the Afghan/Soviet war, the CIA-funded Tora Bora complex, would become a key operational center for Osama bin Laden during the events of 911.

Michael Scheuer, the former head of the CIA's bin Laden unit and the author of Imperial Hubris, told the New York Times that when "Osama lost his father when he was young, and Khalis became a substitute father figure to him ... Bin Laden, along with his four wives and 20-some children, moved into the well-fortified Khalis family compound nine years ago and then to a farm on the outskirts of Jalalabad" (Weaver 2005).

Scheuer went on to indicate that Osama bin Laden immediately began to customize Tora Bora for his family and his key aides and another bunker complex called Milawa for his fighters and as a command center and logistics hub. "By the time bin Laden moved to Kandahar [then a Taliban stronghold] in May of 1997, the two mountain redoubts had been completely refurbished and modernized: they were there, just waiting for him in 2001" (Weaver 2005).

Even being armed with all this knowledge of Khalis and bin Laden, the Pentagon had devised no plan to wage an assault on Tora Bora when they knew bin Laden was cornered there. They ended up sending in a special forces unit of a dozen men, and outsourced the rest of the job to Afghan warlords. Washington's idea of hunting bin Laden was to throw even more money at disloyal warlords to do what carpet bombing the world's most fortified mountain hideouts would obviously not be able to do.

Why didn't the Bush administration make a serious commitment to get the man, who, they say, was responsible for 911? They had him. He was there for the taking. The Bush administration knew that Khalis and bin Laden were like father and son. They knew that the warlords of Afghanistan considered Osama bin Laden a hero. The White House and the CIA knew full well that all of these Afghan warlords hated America, and still they chose to throw away big money on these guys. You need to think about stuff like this when the Republicans in Congress start getting stingy on Medicare and school lunches.

According to an article by Philip Smucker entitled "How Osama bin Laden Got Away" in the Christian Science Monitor, bin Laden gave one hell of a speech at the Jalalabad Islamic studies center to a thousand or so regional tribal leaders, vowing to teach the Americans "a lesson, the same one we taught the Russians" (Smucker 2002). I wonder, are we learning anything?

Now I ask you, do you believe President Bush when he said, "You know, I just don't spend that much time on him?" I certainly do, because the soldiers let him get away, along with an estimated 800 al-Qaeda fighters. If a Democrat had said something like that, the media would have had a field day. President Kennedy was roasted in the press for making a mess of the Bay of Pigs. But he faced the music and said, "This administration intends to be candid about its errors" (Kennedy 1961).

It's too bad that the Bush administration and military brass has been reluctant to be completely candid about its errors. After the debacle at Tora Bora, instead of admitting they blew it and redoubling their efforts to get bin Laden, they tried to defend their decision not to commit adequate forces to the Tora Bora campaign. The President, the Vice President, and General Tommy Franks stated that they were uncertain whether or not Osama bin Laden was even in Tora Bora in December 2001. In an article in the New York Times, General Franks said, "We don't know to this day whether Mr. bin Laden was at Tora Bora," and that bin Laden was "never within our grasp" (Weaver 2005).

Based upon subsequent documents released under the Freedom of Information Act, we now know Tommy Franks either didn't know what he was talking about, or he was lying. The documents reveal that Pentagon investigators did believe bin Laden was at Tora Bora and that he escaped.

In my opinion, if Osama bin Laden instigated 911, then this was not only the biggest miscalculation and mistake since that time, but one of the greatest tactical blunders in the history of modern warfare. This is another example of where the Right went wrong on national security.

But to be sure, there have been too many other missteps to mention along the way in prosecuting this so-called war on terror. Time will not allow me to fully discuss how we allowed A.Q. Khan to make Pakistan a nuclear power and virtually ensure that the spread of atomic weapons can't be stopped.

Permit me to point to an Internet article entitled "The U.S. Knew of A.Q. Khan's Network for Years." The article states,

> The U.S. knew of a network of nuclear proliferation from Pakistan for at least seven years before it was exposed, according to a report. American, British, and UN investigators found that a company in Pakistan was prepared to sell everything needed to make a nuclear bomb — plans, equipment, and fuel — for $50 million, with no questions asked about how it might be used, it said (The Economic Times 2004).

The package was even advertised at a Pakistani arms show in 2000, where the company handed out brochures to visitors, including a reporter for a defense weekly. The company gave out two very glossy brochures, inside of which they promised to provide all of the components needed for a uranium-enrichment facility.

ABC News quoted reporter Andrew Koch as saying behind the program was the now-disgraced Abdul Qadeer Khan, father of Pakistan's nuclear program, who confessed last month to selling nuclear secrets to Iran, North Korea, and Libya. Investigators said he made millions running the operation.

"I think that now we have to confront the reality that there's a nuclear black market, a Wal-Mart, in effect, of nuclear smuggling, and it covers four continents, a dozen countries, and lots of inventive behavior" (The Economic Times 2004), said Graham Allison, director of Harvard University's Center for Science and International Affairs.

Another mistake is to threaten additional wars while we are still bogged down in Iraq and Afghanistan. Should the Bush administration continue moving toward initiating two more wars, one with Iran and one with North Korea, it will overstretch an already overburdened military. Since the military is so severely overstretched, the administration is revamping strategic doctrine to allow for "preventative nuclear attacks." This is a radical shift away from the nuclear doctrine of deterrence and has the potential to initiate a new arms race.

The Pentagon document "Doctrine for Joint Nuclear Operations" calls for the use of nuclear weapons against non-nuclear adversaries in order "to ensure success of U.S. and multinational operations" (Declassified draft under direction of Gen. Richard B. Meyers 2006). But a newspaper article by Walter Pincus tells us,

Arms control specialists and others have criticized the draft. Some say formally planning to use nuclear weapons preemptively increases the likelihood they will be used. Others said endorsement of preemptive strikes will make it tougher to persuade non-nuclear nations to forgo building an atomic arsenal (Pincus 2005).

Iran and North Korea are familiar with this shift in strategic nuclear doctrine in America. This radical doctrinal shift in strategic nuclear posture, combined with the signal from the U.S. in preemptively attacking the only completely non-nuclear component of the so-called Axis of Evil, is enough to keep Iran and North Korea working on their nuclear programs. Not to mention the fact that Iranian momentum towards nuclear development is uniting an Iran that has previously been bearish on their new President Ahmadinejad.

It is my sincere prayer that the kinds of battlefield or tactical nuclear weapons that are mentioned in Bush's Nuclear Posture Review will never be used. I hope that the Bush administration can find a way to deal with Iran without choosing a preemptive nuclear strike, because the ripple effect would be nearly untenable, to say the least.

Don't forget that China gets about 60 percent of its oil from Iran. Therefore, a preemptive nuclear strike against Iran by the United States or Israel would probably push an already low-intensity confrontational relationship between China and the West over the edge.

That kind of thing would not only devastate the global economy, but it would leave the U.S. totally isolated and possibly galvanize the entire Islamic world against us. We could even very possibly see the Shiites unite with the Sunnis in Iraq against the U.S. and Israel.

Now after three years into the conflict in Iraq, we have certainly had enough time to assess some of the missteps, miscalculations, and blunders made along the way. One of the biggest mistakes in the prosecution of the war is that the Pentagon and the American people have not properly understood the enemy. We were told, we're taking the fight to the enemy. We're fighting them over there so we don't have to face them here. The idea was to draw terrorists into Iraq so we could kill them there.

But 98 percent of the armed opposition to U.S. forces is Iraqi, and only 2 percent are outsiders. America faces an insurgency in Iraq, not outsiders like al-Qaeda coming into the country. Therein lies the problem; the Bush administration did not expect this kind of insurgency.

In a September 2005 Time magazine article entitled "Saddam's Revenge," by Joe Klein, a retired four star general told Klein,

> We're good at fighting armies, but we don't know how to do this. We don't have enough intelligence analysts working on this problem. The Defense Intelligence Agency puts most of its emphasis and its assets on Iran, North Korea, and China. The Iraqi insurgency is simply not a top priority, and that's a damn shame (Klein 2005).

Today, intelligence experts believe the insurgency's support infrastructure, their finances, pay schedules, and logistics networks were planned before, in anticipation of a U.S. invasion. They also have concluded that the Bush administration's fixation on finding WMD allowed the insurgency to become fully galvanized and entrenched. They are now telling us that it has been extremely difficult to develop a counter-insurgency strategy because of the frequent replacement of U.S. military and administrative resources. As unbelievable as it seems, we are repeating the same mistakes we made in Vietnam with Ho Chi Minh's insurgency.

Klein tells us of three major tactical blunders of the Bush administration in Iraq. The first was in April of 2003, when General Tommy Franks decided to take an inadequately small number of troops to Baghdad very quickly. He wanted to hurry into Baghdad so Bush could do his photo op by May 1st and declare the end of major combat operations. Franks himself also had plans to return to Tampa.

But what was worse than the rush job was allowing Lt. General David McKiernan and his operation of several hundred intelligence officers to follow Franks out of Iraq. That was one of the biggest mistakes of the Iraq war. Franks and McKiernan's departure left only a couple dozen intelligence officers in Iraq to figure out whom, what, when, and where the enemy was.

Operation Iraqi Freedom used the threat of terrorism the way that preceding NSCs used the threat of Communism to implement regime change. This time, however, the ousted dictator, Saddam Hussein, left the country set up perfectly for a formidable insurgent campaign against the United States.

But having said that, I now wonder if General Franks was sufficiently concerned about stockpiled weapons found in the march to Baghdad. Evidently not, because these huge stockpiles of weapons were left largely unsecured. Now, many of those weapons are in the hands of the insurgency.

The second major tactical blunder occurred on May 23, 2005, when Donald Rumsfeld ordered the chief administrator of the Coalitional Provisional Authority, Paul Bremer, to disband the Iraqi army and the Iraqi Civil Service. Thousands of these ignored assets shifted into the insurgency, taking with them: the knowledge of tactical weapons, Iraq's electrical grid, water system, and sewer system.

Didn't we learn anything from Operation Paperclip? Bremer said he didn't regret it because "We had bombed their barracks and didn't know how to separate the good from the bad, and we didn't have enough troops to stop the looting in Baghdad" (Weaver 2005). That's what happens when you don't have a plan.

The third major tactical blunder was the decision in spring 2003 to make WMD search the top intelligence priority. Ambassador Joe Wilson told the Bush administration that there were no WMD in Iraq The world told them the same thing. Still, the Bush administration's myopic focus was on WMD. They sent David Kay and 1,200 intelligence officials into Iraq in June 2003 on a wild goose chase.

On top of all that, Kay was holding thousands of pages of intelligence from Saddam's office. Why didn't he offer to help the military with information contained in those documents about the insurgency? Some of the intelligence

Kay had was invaluable on things like Saddam's military support resources, Saddam's analysts, translators, and field agents. This was indispensable information on what our troops would have to face.

What did Kay do? He ordered his intelligence officials to stop working with sources on the Iraqi insurgency. If a source was working on WMD, Kay didn't see the value in accumulating and assessing their intelligence in matters pertaining to the Iraqi insurgency.

Neither was the Bush administration interested in wasting time trying to get a bead on the insurgency. When it came to maps of weapons caches, the whereabouts of key Baathists and their safe houses, evidently this information was of very little interest to the Bush camp. When it came to some 38 boxes of documents on Fallujah, Samarra, and Ramadi marked "No Intelligence Value," the Bush administration didn't see the value in them either. Even their full knowledge that Fallujah, particularly, was a hotbed of Sunni rebellion wasn't enough to get a rise out of these guys.

The cavalier attitude of the Bush administration and the way they handled this intelligence clearly contributed to their misjudgments about the enemy. It is said that hindsight is 20/20. But it doesn't take hindsight for anyone to see these obvious blunders clearer than Hubble sees the moon.

Achieving Stability in Iraq

Now that the Bush administration has unilaterally taken this nation to war in Iraq, it is my hope that the

President does not underestimate the need to internationalize the approaching post-war phase in Iraq. This will require exquisite statecraft and a sober, pragmatic approach. The entire Middle East and the rest of the world should be made to see the incentives, both strategic and economic, in having a stable and politically healthy Iraq at peace with its neighbors. The American people must remain engaged in constant debate in these matters to ensure that any gaps in judgment within the executive branch will be filled.

One way of achieving the international consensus we seek in Iraq is to begin discussing the post-war phase of this project in Iraq. Such discussion must include the eventual de-Americanization of the project. Washington owes it to the American people, especially those with a little skin in the game, to begin outlining an exit strategy well ahead of the actual period of withdrawal. Now is a good time since Iraq has held elections to establish a permanent government. The Bush administration should view the recent success with referendums and elections in Iraq as stepping-stones toward Iraqization of this project and an ultimate U.S. withdrawal.

Please don't misunderstand me. Just because there have been elections in Iraq doesn't mean there is a weakening of the insurgency. It is precisely our presence in Iraq that fuels the insurgency. As long as we are there, the insurgents can point to our occupation of Iraq and use it as a recruitment tool. The evidence shows that U.S. forces are a major factor contributing to Iraq's instability and an obstacle to the process of national reconciliation. Polls consistently show that some 80 percent of Iraqis want us to leave. Therefore, I believe that the insurgency will last as long as U.S. troops are occupying Iraq.

What do U.S. military experts say about it? I agree with Representative John Murtha when he said our troops have become "a catalyst for violence" (Murtha 2005). Top U.S. military commanders have even agreed. They also admit that this, and any other insurgency, cannot be defeated militarily.

Now I must mention the geostrategic importance of withdrawal. Syria and Iran hoped to bleed America dry, like the Mujahideen did to the Soviets in Afghanistan. They are hoping the United States' actions in Iraq will weaken its larger hegemonic influence in the region.

Contrary to what many people think, the chief perpetrators of violence in Iraq, notwithstanding the U.S. military, are not terrorists being drawn into the country from outside Iraq. Nor are they foreign fighters associated with Abu Musab al-Zarqawi, who called the election the Devil's work and threatened anyone who voted. But the violence comes from an internal insurgency.

Note how Zarqawi couldn't carry out his threats. I'm sure he wanted to stop the election, but he couldn't. No matter what the American media says, the fact that nothing happened should show you how little of a military threat he really is.

It seems to me that once the United States withdraws, al-Qaeda would be stupid to try anything in Iraq because Iraqi nationalists, and even the insurgents, would likely pounce on them. Insurgent leaders have already told Arab League officials at the league's November conference that they would turn Zarqawi over to Iraqi authorities. Heaven help Zarqari's followers if the Iraqi military got them; they would go to jail or be shot.

What the elections do mean, however, is another step toward sovereignty for the Iraqi people. What it should mean for our troops is one more step towards coming home. What it should mean for the taxpayers of the U.S. is a few less dollars to pay for the installation of a radical Shiite religious regime.

In the final analysis, the Iraqi people must be able to stand on their own and govern themselves. That's what they must be told, and I believe that's the only way we can bring our troops home in any significant numbers.

But evidently the Bush administration and the political Right in America can't see this, because they continue to characterize any talk of withdrawal as yellow belly liberal cutting and running. Cutting and running is not what I'm talking about. I'm talking about shifting Iraq from being an exclusively American problem toward a regional and international pragmatic solution. As long as the world and the Middle East can sit back and watch, they will. Iraq's neighbors must be made to contribute to the stability of the region in a way that is not parasympathetic to American interests.

At the same time, the United States can't continue to ignore the efforts and solutions offered by the Arab League. Secretary of State Condoleezza Rice should have attended their conference in Cairo this past November. This is the only way to limit the chances of increased sectarian violence and further degeneration of Iraq into civil war.

A constructive and nurturing international and regional influence is the best approach to mitigating the disputes over a great many issues in Iraq, including the federalization of its oil. The world must convince the Shiite majority in Iraq, through incentives, and, if necessary, some form of sanctions, that insuring the Sunni minority an egalitarian share of Iraq's great wealth is absolutely essential. The United States, alone, cannot accomplish this diplomatic task for various sociopolitical reasons. Maybe that's why it appears that we aren't really trying.

For all these reasons, we need an exit strategy in Iraq. Congress must give the Bush administration a time limit on its strategy. I say, and you can quote me on this one: "If America can't afford an activist government on behalf of its working class, then we can't afford to support the Shiites as peacekeepers in a civil war." Now is the time for those who are honest about this war to man up.

Now is the time for Congress to man up. Congress must make any future funding for Iraq contingent on establishing a clear-cut deadline for withdrawal. A withdrawal must be used as a diplomatic tool. It is THE method of ending the insurgency and ending the specter of civil war in Iraq. Civil war in Iraq has a high probability of drawing in the region's other powers. In other words, it's time to take the damn training wheels off.

It's also time to sober up and take stock of what we have done in the name of national security. When we do that, we will see that the Iraq war has cost more than 2,100 American lives, more than 16,000 American kids are wounded, and some are maimed for life, and thousands of Iraqis are now dead. Our military has become demoralized, overstretched, and weakened. This administration and its war of choice has so damaged America's standing in the world, that internationalizing the Iraq project has become nearly impossible. We have become willing to say goodbye to our civil liberties and given away our precious resources that we so badly need for ourselves.

The Iraqi war has become the single most dangerous threat to our national security. It has totally destroyed our standing in the world as Reagan's "shining city upon the hill" (Reagan 1989). It has become our generation's most epic tragedy.

Now there are those who will rightfully say that the attacks of September 11, 2001 were an epic tragedy too. But the devastation caused by the attack itself pales in comparison to the loss of human life and the financial cost that has resulted from the Bush administration's ad hoc and inappropriate response. Millions of lives are still potentially at stake.

According to Nobel Prize-winning economist Joseph Stiglitz, conservatively, $2 trillion will be spent fighting a single war we shouldn't be fighting. This is money that could have been better spent on domestic issues like the environment, jobs, health care, and education.

Not only that, this war has the potential to lead to other wars, and those wars could likely lead to further terrorist attacks. This whole thing can escalate without end. So if we make bad decisions, we can kick off a death spiral of devastation, in which the more we fight it — the worse it gets. We could, literally, become our own worst enemy and aid in the destruction of our way of life — all in the name of national security.

Conclusion

★ ★ ★ ★ ★

Franklin Roosevelt once told the American people, "The only thing we have to fear is fear itself" (Roosevelt 1933). If we have become so afraid that we are willing to sacrifice the rule of law and allow this continued rise of an imperial presidency in America, then the terrorists have won. They will have successfully convinced America to attack itself.

What do I mean? I mean to say that the Constitution of the United States was written, not to protect us from foreign armies — it was written to protect us from ourselves. The Constitution establishes the core value of America, its freedom.

The question is, are we willing, in the name of national security, to sacrifice our freedoms by rendering the U.S. Constitution irrelevant?

When we allow fear to cause us to compromise the Constitution and give up the very thing that has tempered the will of the few in their drive to advance an agenda that excludes the will of the many, we have placed ourselves on the high road to tyranny. As Bill Moyers said,

> Thus the President was given no power to authorize private war, whether declared or undeclared, whether fought with regular public forces or by buccaneers and soldiers of fortune. The Declaration of war was to be a public and collegial act — in no small part because in a republic, those who will the end must also will the means of the end, accepting responsibility for the consequences of their choices (Moyers 1988).

Already, we have seen a very antidemocratic propensity by our government to outsource those war powers reserved to the Congress under the Constitution to the unilateral prerogatives of the presidency. Such was the case during the Iran/Contra period, when the Contras were covertly militarized, and such is the case today with the use of private paramilitary units from Iraq to New Orleans.

As Professor Carroll Quigley said in his classic book Tragedy and Hope, "All of past history shows that the shift from a mass army of citizen soldiers to a smaller army of professional fighters leads, in the long run, to a decline of democracy" (Quigley 1966).

In other words, whenever Congress bans military action, various presidents have invoked their unilateral privileges under the framework of the National Security Act to do an end-run around the will of the Congress. By whatever means at their disposal, various presidents have used both citizen and private armies, counterfeit mobs, proxy forces, and so forth to carry out secret operations without sufficient regard for the Constitution, the will of Congress, and the will of the American people.

Those aspects of the National Security Act that appear to work against the Constitution should be revisited if we intend not to become a purveyor of impulsive power in the world and ultimately set ourselves up for further attacks.

Because of this arbitrary way we chose to exercise our standing as leaders of the free world, the world has grown increasingly dubious about America. Now, other countries are afraid of us. If we allow our neighbors to remain afraid of us, it will make diplomacy that much harder, and the option of advancing U.S. foreign policy through the use of carrots will slowly be replaced by the stick. Saber rattling will begin to take the place of the conference table, and dread will become our epithet.

What has generated this drive toward overt authoritarianism at home and apparent thuggery and callousness in our foreign affairs? The answer is, we do it because we can.

In a book called Of Paradise and Power: America and Europe in the New World Order by Robert Kagan, we are reminded that no other nation successfully built such a military superstate the way America did after World War II. The Soviets tried and failed. They were undone by the stress of their own imperial overstretch. Europe, on the other hand, decided upon peace through an economic cooperative dynamic. But America has chosen to leverage its foreign policies by having the biggest military stick in the history of the modern world. Quigley tells us,

> ... when a period can be dominated by complex and expensive weapons that only a few persons can afford to possess or can learn to use, we have a situation where the minority who control such "specialist" weapons can dominate the majority who lack them. In such a society, sooner or later, an authoritarian political system that reflects the inequality in control of weapons will be established (Kagan 2003).

In other words, if you have the world's largest, most powerful, and most far-reaching military, you don't have to walk softly if you choose not to, and sooner or later, you will cease to apply diplomacy altogether.

Since the passage of the National Security Act of 1947, America has increasingly become the home of arbitrary power. This is not what Washington, Madison, and Jefferson were supposed to have prescribed. America was designed to be a country tempered by checks and balances. If one faction within our government broke the rules, there would be a tempering dynamic from the others. President Kennedy said,

> The men who create power make an indispensable contribution to the nation's greatness. But the men who question power make a contribution just as indispensable, especially when that questioning is disinterested. For they determine whether we use power or power uses us (Kennedy 1963).

Since 1947, we have allowed power to use us, and at the same time, we've allowed it to abuse others. Since 911, we have seen a dramatic acceleration of this dynamic. The recent actions of the Republican-controlled government in this country, unauthorized domestic spying, torturing of detainees, the doctrine of preemption, violations of the Geneva Convention's treaties, compromising the Transatlantic Alliance, ignoring the cries for support of democracy in Haiti, the inability to address the border security issue, and the ad hoc removal of assets that used to work toward reducing drug proliferation and security in the Caribbean, have all made America less safe and secure. Now after two decades of the Washington Consensus, our neighbors to the South are forming a unified front against American interests, compromising our national security.

As if the unauthorized domestic spying wasn't enough, a recent article by BBC Pentagon correspondent Adam Brookes entitled "U.S. Plans to Fight the Net Revealed," tells us about big brother taking things a step further. A newly declassified document has revealed that the U.S. military has plans for "information operations" — to encompass psychological operations to attacks on hostile computer networks. Brookes writes,

> Bloggers beware. As the world turns networked, the Pentagon is calculating the military opportunities that computer networks, wireless technologies, and the modern media offer. From influencing public opinion through news media to designing "computer network attack" weapons, the U.S. military is learning to fight an electronic

war. The declassified document is called "Information Operations Roadmap." It was obtained by the National Security Archive at George Washington University using the Freedom of Information Act. Officials in the Pentagon wrote it in 2003. The Secretary of Defense, Donald Rumsfeld, signed it.

The roadmap calls for a far-reaching overhaul of the military's ability to conduct information operations and electronic warfare. And, in some detail, it makes recommendations for how the U.S. armed forces should think about this new, virtual warfare. The document says that information is critical to military success. Computer and telecommunications networks are of vital operational importance (Brookes 2006).

In other words, to the Pentagon, the Internet has become a tactical weapon of sorts. As such, some of us who participate in online dissent could be viewed as an enemy of the state.

In big brother's attempt to fight fire with fire, Brooke says,

The most startling aspect of the roadmap is its acknowledgement that information put out as part of the military's psychological operations, or Psyops, is finding its way onto the computer and television screens of ordinary Americans. "Information intended for foreign audiences, including public diplomacy and Psyops, is increasingly consumed by our domestic audience," it reads. Psyops messages will often be replayed by the news media for much larger audiences, including the American public, it goes on (Brookes 2006).

Yes, today, America's intelligence and military establishment is using much more powerful tools, like the Internet and blogging, created in our modern technological revolution, to officially label Iran and North Korea as rogue states. This is in keeping with the way Nazi Germany, the Soviet Union, Mossadegh's Iran, Guatemala, Chile, and Nicaragua were all painted as antithetical through the use of propaganda in the past.

The labeling of a country as a rogue state can have a relative and nuanced meaning. The use of that epithet has always played a preeminent role in policy planning and national security analysis. But we should remember one point. That is, that just because the United States has labeled Iraq, Iran, and North Korea as rogue states, it does not mean that Washington is not obliged to reasonably exhaust the rules of engagement as established by member nations of the UN Security Council.

The United States should always seek to act in accordance with international laws and treaty obligations. If we ignore the rules and laws that we ask others to follow, then we are no better than a rogue state. The UN's Charter states that,

> The Security Council shall determine the existence of any threat to the peace, breach of the peace, or act of aggression, and shall make recommendations, or decide what measures shall be taken in accordance with Articles 41 and 42,

which detail the preferred measures not involving the use of armed force and permit the Security Council to take further action if it finds such measures inadequate. The only exception is Article 51, which permits the right of individual or collective self-defense against armed attack ... until the Security Council has taken the measures necessary to maintain international peace and security. Apart from these exceptions, member states shall refrain in their international relations from the threat or use of force (Charter of the United Nations 1945).

As Noam Chomsky said,

There are legitimate ways to react to the many threats to world peace. If Iraq's neighbors feel threatened, they can approach the Security Council to authorize appropriate measures to respond to the threat. If the U.S. and Britain feel threatened, they can do the same. But no state has the authority to make its own determinations on these matters and to act as it chooses; the U.S. and UK would have no such authority even if their own hands were clean, hardly the case (Chomsky 1998).

Let's just keep it real for a moment. If the U.S. can deem the UN irrelevant and unilaterally invade Iraq under false intelligence assessments, how can we then say to Hamas, for example, because you have used terrorism in the past against Israel, we consider you are a rogue state, and, therefore, diplomatic engagement with the West is not possible?

Or, if the Reagan administration sold Iraqi President Saddam Hussein weaponized anthrax and bubonic plague, and at the same time sold arms to the Iranians, while knowing Iraq and Iran were at war with each other, then how can we label any country a rogue state or charge them with proliferating WMD?

If the Nixon administration could use so-called spoiling operations to illegally influence the outcome of free and democratic elections in Chile, how can we turn around and say that Saddam Hussein is an oppressor of his people and rigs his elections?

If the Eisenhower administration allowed the CIA to create counterfeit mobs and proxy armies to overthrow the Mossadegh government in Iran and the Arbenz government in Guatemala under false pretenses, how can we accuse any other country that threatens its neighbors of government lawlessness? The answers to these simple, but yet complex questions is — we can't.

While serving as Secretary of State under President Clinton, Madeleine Albright informed the UN Security Council during an earlier U.S. confrontation with Iraq that the U.S. intends to act "multilaterally when we can and unilaterally as we must." She also said that, "We recognize this area as vital to U.S. national interests" (Chomsky 1998).

In other words, there would be no external constraint whenever the U.S. deemed it not to be strategically expedient. The international order could, therefore, be defined by the whims of American nihilism.

When UN Secretary-General Kofi Annan undertook his February 1998 diplomatic mission to Iraq, Secretary of State Albright said, "When he comes back, we will see what he has brought and how it fits with our national interests" (Chomsky 1998).

In other words, America's response would not be determined by international law, but by whether or not Annan was successful with concessions from abroad. Albright repeated America's unilateral view of keeping the international order: "It is possible that he will come with something we don't like, in which case, we will pursue our national interests" (Chomsky 1998).

President Clinton warned that if Iraq fails in conformity to Washington's demands, " ... everyone would understand that then the United States and, hopefully, all of our allies would have the unilateral right to respond at a time, place, and manner of our own choosing" (Chomsky 1998).

Listening to our leaders, it seems that, somehow, an American response that breaks the established rules of engagement as set forth by the UN Security Council is not equated in Washington with other violent and lawless states breaking the rules. According to the statements of the Secretary of State at that time, one gets the impression that our dirt would have been seen as somehow cleaner than the dirt of others. I call it diplomatic exceptionalism.

What we have been witnessing in America since the passage of the National Security Act of 1947 is not only a constitutional crisis, but also a crisis of our national soul. It is my humble prayer that the lessons of this book can be internalized and practically applied before it's too late. I'm reminded of when the Messiah sat on the Mount of Olives, and his disciples came to Him privately, saying,

> "Tell us, when will these things be? And what will be the sign of your coming, and of the end of the age?" Yahshua [Jesus] answered and said to them: "Take heed that no one deceives you. For many will come in my name, saying, 'I am the Christ,' and will deceive many" (Bible).

I believe a principle was being illustrated in that statement. What do I mean? Based on the definition of the word "name," meaning "the reputation of someone or something," many will appear to have a righteous intent, but their motivations are actually the opposite. Similarly, many people have been deceived into giving their consent to disruptive, unwise, and antidemocratic U.S. actions abroad — in the name of national security. In the Sermon on the Mount, Jesus also told his disciples,

> And you will hear of wars and rumors of wars. See that you are not troubled, for all these things must come to pass, but the end is not yet. For nation will rise against nation, and kingdom against kingdom. And there will be famines, pestilences, and earthquakes in various places. All these are the beginning of sorrows (Bible).

In my book, *Thieves in the Temple: America Under the Federal Reserve System*, I explained how banks make money. They do it by collecting interest on debts. Remember, nothing generates debt like war. So long as war continues to be such a profitable business, we will hear of "wars and rumors of wars," and "nations rising against nations."

It is sad, however, that people are afraid to speak out about the havoc created in the name of national security. But the Messiah also spoke about the assassination of the body and character of those who stand up and speak out for what's right. He said, "Then they will deliver you up to tribulation and kill you, and you will be hated by all nations for My name's sake. And then many will be offended, will betray one another, and will hate one another" (Bible).

When President Bush was asked who was his most admired historical figure and philosopher, he answered, "Christ, because He changed my heart" (Bush 1999). Our President claims to be a man of faith, but sometimes his actions make me wonder. How can you claim to follow the teachings of Christ, and then preemptively and unilaterally attack a country based upon lies or miscalculations without acknowledging contrition over the affair? Some claim to be led by Christ, but, in fact, are really led by something else. The Messiah summed it up, "Then many false prophets will rise up and deceive many" (Bible).

The Messiah speaks about those who seem to remain indifferent toward the lawless, dishonorable, and deceptive actions undertaken in the name of national security, and those who choose to rationalize and justify the suffering of the innocent as unavoidable collateral damage from the kinds of covert actions abroad that I have discussed in this book when He said, "And because lawlessness will abound, the love of many will grow cold" (Bible).

If righteousness is our creed, then let us work to maintain our fidelity to that principle. Let us proceed in the light with all deliberate tolerance toward others. Let those on the Left who say, "I'm for the little guy," endure in all sincerity. Let those on the Right who say, "I'm for moral values," hold steadfast and keep their representatives mindful of that charge. If we pursue peace and true justice and do not falter, then we will prevail. As the Messiah put it, "... he who endures to the end shall be saved" (Bible).

Finally, until we see heaven and hell as spiritual and psychological states of consciousness, not as geographical locations, we will continue missing the lessons of the Sermon on the Mount, particularly as they relate to the constitutional crisis in America under the national security state. The lessons applied here say: If deceit, murder, greed, avarice, callousness, and war abide within one's consciousness, then that person's abode is in darkness and hell. The only thing that will extinguish the darkness in the hearts of man is the righteous substance of spirit — the love of truth, honesty, chastity, charity, and goodwill.

It is my hope that my preaching and exposing of where the Right went wrong on national security, and the Left too, will help bring about the end of at least this one aspect of the inward world of mental darkness and hell on earth. We must want to build a kingdom of light as our dwelling place (heaven within) or remain in a kingdom of lies, deceit, and death (hell within).

To me, this is the kingdom of heaven that the Bible speaks of, and the One we should seek. We should be glad to see the old world of greed and strife within our hearts pass away and look forward to the birth of a new world of peace within our hearts. As the Messiah said, "And this gospel of the kingdom will be preached in all the world as a witness to all the nations, and then the end will come" (Bible). May the Keeper of heaven and earth bless us all with understanding.

References

Abrahamian, Ervand. 1993. Khomeinism: Essays on the Islamic Republic. Berkeley, CA: University of California Press.

Albright, Madeline. 2000. "Address to the American-Iranian Council." The New York Times.

Bearden, Milton. 2002. "Hunting bin Laden." PBS Frontline, a co-production with the New York Times and Rain Media Inc., November.

The Bible: King James Version. The Book of Matthew, Chapter 24:1–14.

Blum, William. 1995. Killing Hope: U.S. Military and CIA Interventions since World War II. Monroe, Maine: Common Courage Press.

Braun, Carol Mosley. 2004. South Florida Speaks Out. Miami, WSRF 1580 AM.

Brookes, Adam. 2006. "U.S. Plans to Fight the Net Revealed." BBC News, January 27.

Bush, George W. 1999. "Televised Republican Presidential Debates." CSPAN, Des Moines, Iowa, December 13.

Bush, George W. 2001. "Presidential Address to the Nation." Office of the Press Secretary, Washington, D.C., September 11.

Bush, George W. 2002. "Presidential Press Conference." Office of the Press Secretary, Washington, D.C., March 13.

Bush, George W. 2002. "State of the Union Address." Office of the Press Secretary. Washington, D.C., January 20.

Cabib, Leila. 2000. "Balancing Act: Can America Sustain a Population of 500 Million — Or Even a Billion — by 2100?" Marion, Ohio: E-Magazine, November/December.

Charter of the United Nations. 1945. "Action With Respect to Threats to the Peace, Breaches of the Peace, and Acts of Aggression." San Francisco, CA: United Nations, June 26, Chapter 7, Articles 41, 42, 51.

Chietigj Bajpaee. 2005. "Chinese Energy Strategy in Latin America." Washington, D.C.: The Jamestown Foundation, Volume 5, Issue 14, June 21.

Chomsky, Noam. 1998. "Rogue States." Z-Magazine. Woods Hole, MA, April.

Chronology of Key Public Events, http://www.fas.org/irp/offdocs/walsh/chron.htm (accessed 1/25/06).

Cole, Carleton. Christian Science Monitor, May 27, 1999, p. 23.

Declassified draft under direction of Gen. Richard B. Meyers. 2006. "Doctrine for Joint Nuclear Operations." Washington, D.C.: Pentagon.

Doyle, Kate, and Peter Kornbluh. 1997. "Declassified: CIA and Assassinations: The Guatemala 1954 Documents." Washington, D.C.: The National Security Archive.

The Economic Times. 2004. "The U.S. Knew of A.Q. Khan's Network for Years." Bennett, Coleman and Company, March 5.

Emergencies and Response: Emphasis on Local Response. 2002. "National Response Plan." Washington, D.C., May 29.

Europe News Poll. 2003. "The Biggest Threat to Peace." Time Europe. London, England.

Ferguson, Charles D. 2004. Can Bush or Kerry Prevent Nuclear Terrorism? Council on Foreign Relations. http://www.cfr.org/publication/ 7305/can_bush_or_kerry_ prevent_nuclear_ terrorism.html Washington, D.C., September (accessed 2/2/06).

Fitts, Catherine Austin. 2004. South Florida Speaks Out. WSRF 1580 AM, Miami, Fl., October.

Higham, Charles. 1983. Trading with the Enemy: The Nazi American Money Plot 1933–1949. New York: Delacorte Press.

Hosmer, Stephen T. 2001. Operations Against Enemy Leaders. Santa Monica, CA: Rand.

Kagan, Robert. 2003. Of Paradise and Power: America and Europe in the New World Order. New York: Random House.

Kennedy, John F. 1961. Inaugural Address. http://www.bartleby.com/124/ pres56.html (accessed 1/4/06).

Kennedy, John F. 1961. "Presidential Address Before the American Newspaper Publishers Association." New York: John F. Kennedy Library, April 27.

Kennedy, John F. 1963. "Speech at Amherst College." Boston, Mass.: JFK Library. October 19.

Kinzer, Stephen. 2003. All the Shah's Men: An American Coup and The Roots of Middle East Terror. Hoboken, N.J.: John Wiley & Sons, Inc. 1st edition.

Klein, Joe. 2005. "Saddam's Revenge." Time Magazine, September 26.

Lardy, Nicholas R. 2002. Integrating China into the Global Economy. Washington, D.C.: The Brookings Institution.

Lasby, Clare. 1975. "Operation Paperclip." New York: Athenaeum.

LaTulippe, Steven. 2005. America, Iran, and Operation Ajax: The Burden of the Past. http://www.lewrockwell. com/latulippe/ latulippe41.html (accessed 1/4/06).

Lehrer, Jim. 2005. The Threat of Nuclear Terrorism, http://www.pbs.org/ newshour/bb/international/proliferation/terroris_threat.html (accessed 2/1/06).

Liggio, Leonard P. "Oil and American Foreign Policy," Libertarian Review, July/August 1979.

Mackler, Jeff. 2005 Lockheed, the King of Warfare. Lockheed, the King of Warfare JEFF MACKLER / Socialist Action 1feb2005 (accessed 2/17/06).

Moyers, Bill. 1987. "The Secret Government: The Constitution in Crises," PBS Documentary.

Moyers, Bill. 1988. The Secret Government: The Constitution in Crises. Washington, D.C.: Seven Locks Press, p. 28.

Murawiec, Laurent. 2002. "Briefing Depicted Saudis as Enemies." Washington Post, August 6.

Murtha, John. 2005. "Congressman Murtha calls for redeployment from Iraq." Washington, D.C.: U.S. House of Representatives, November 17.

Nelson-Pallmeyer, Jack. 1992. Brave New World Order. New York: Orbis Books, Maryknoll.

Osama bin Laden. 2006. "Osama bin Laden Speaks." Al-Jazeera Television. Doha, Qatar, January 19.

Phillips, David Atlee. 1977. The Night Watch: 25 Years of Peculiar Service. New York: Atheneum.

Pincus, Walter. 2005. "Pentagon May Have Doubts about Preemptive Nuclear Move." Washington Post, September 19, Page A05.

Pipes, Daniel. 2002/03. "The Scandal of U.S.-Saudi Relations." National Interest, http://www.danielpipes.org/article/995 (accessed 2-2-06).

Powell, Bill. 2001. "China's Great Step Forward; Get Ready for the Biggest Coming Out Party in the History of Capitalism: China's Formal Accession to the WTO. Here's How the Global Economy Is Going to Change," Fortune Magazine, September 17.

Quigley, Carroll. 1966. Tragedy and Hope. New York: Macmillan Company.

Reagan, Ronald. 1987. "Press Conference with Pope John Paul II." Washington, D.C.: National Archives, September 10.

Reagan, Ronald. 1989. "Farewell Address to the Nation." Simi Valley, CA: Ronald Reagan Library, January 19.

Reed, Terry, and John Cummings. 1995. Compromised: Clinton, Bush and the CIA. Granite Bay, CA: Clandestine Publishing.

Richman, Sheldon L. "Policy Analysis: The United States and the Persian Gulf," Cato Policy Analysis No. 46, January 10, 1985.

Roosevelt, Franklin. 1933. "First Inaugural Address." Washington, D.C.: National Archives, March 4.

Roush, Patricia M. 2002. "Committee on Government Reform, U.S. House of Representatives." Washington, D.C.: U.S. House of Representatives, June 12, p. 3.

Rutz, Carol. 2005. A Nation Betrayed. Grass Lake, Minnesota: Fidelity Publishing.

Sapheri, Saman. 2002. "The Geopolitics of Oil." The International Socialist Review, November/December.

Smucker, Philip, 2002. "How Osama bin Laden Got Away." The Christian Science Monitor, March 4.

Spartacus Educational. "Jaboco Arbenz," http://www.spartacus. schoolnet.co.uk/JFKarbenz.htm (accessed 2/2/06).

Staff. 2004. "The Passing of the Buck," The Economist Newspaper Limited, December 2.

Staff report of the Select Committee to Study Governmental Operations with Respect to Intelligence Activities. 1975. "Covert Action in Chile 1963–1973." U.S. Senate, December 18.

Tariq Ali. 2003. The Clash of Fundamentalisms: Crusades, Jihads, and Modernity. New York: Verso.

U.S. House of Representatives Appropriations Bill. 1982. "The Boland Amendment." Washington, D.C.

Weaver, Mary Anne. 2005. "Lost at Tora Bora." New York Times, September 11.

Weiner, Tim. 1997. "CIA's Openness Derided as a 'Snow Job.'" New York Times. May 20.

Weiner, Tim. 2004. "Lockheed, the Future of Warfare." New York Times, Nov. 28. http://www.lewrockwell.com/latulippe/latulippe41.html.

Wilber, Donald N. 1954. Clandestine Service History: Overthrow of Premier Mossadeq of Iran November 1952–August 1953. http://www.nytimes. com/library/world/mideast/041600iran-cia-index.html.

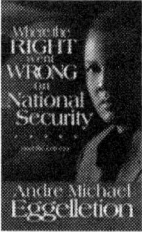

BOOKS AVAILABLE THROUGH
Milligan Books, Inc.

Where The Right Went Wrong On National Security - $14.95
Thieves In The Temple - $14.95

Order Form
Milligan Books, Inc.
1425 W. Manchester Ave., Suite C
Los Angeles, CA 90047
(323) 750-3592

Name _____

Address _____

City _____ State _____ Zip _____

Day & Evening Tele _____

Email _____

Please check boxes:

☐ **Where The Right Went Wrong**-$14.95 ... *Quantity* _____ $ _____

☐ **Thieves In The Temple**-$14.95 .... *Quantity* _____ $ _____

Sales Tax (California add 8.25%) .... $ _____

Shipping & handling $5.95 for 1st book .... $ _____

Add $1.00 for each additional book .... $ _____

TOTAL AMOUNT DUE .... $ _____

☐ Visa ☐ M/C ☐ AMEX ☐ Discover ☐ Check ☐ Money Order

Credit Card # _____ Exp. Date _____

_____
Signature   Date

Make check payable to Milligan Books, Inc.